LUBO: A Life Less Ordinary

By

Michal Zeman and Joe Sullivan

CONTENTS

I dedicate this book to my father. He did not live to see me at the top of my career but he made a most significant contribution to it.

LUBOMIR MORAVCIK
October 2001

Published by Celtic Football Club.

Designed & produced by Grange Communications Ltd, Edinburgh.
Printed in EU

ISBN: 1-902704-27-4

ACKNOWLEDGEMENTS

Paul Cuddihy and Siobhan McBean at Celtic Football Club.
Scott Munro at First Press Publishing.
Translation of Slovakian text by Vladimir Alexa.

FOREWORD

I first met Lubo just before we played Leipzig in a pre-season friendly in Germany. He had joined our party almost directly from holiday and so he was a long way off being match fit. So, to help his fitness as well as getting a look at his ability, I put him in a left wing back role. Now, Lubo Moravcik is a multi-talented footballer but one thing I learned very quickly indeed – he cannot play wing back.

I had a few strong words for him at the end of a poor evening but I detected in him a determination to prove to any new manager something that he had already demonstrated to thousands at Celtic Park in the recent past – that he was a very gifted footballer indeed!! And during the course of the season he did precisely that.

As the weeks and months rolled by, I naturally got to know Lubo a little better than before. He was 35-years-old but looked at least 10 years younger. I often joked with him that he had wasted this great natural talent that very few footballers possessed but he just smiled back and said that he had been entertaining fans all over France for the past decade, where he had played much of his club football.

Because of his age he couldn't play every game – although he probably thought he could – and so, last season, I used him for many big matches but tried to give him some extra rest.

I also think he found the amount of training he had to do was just to his liking and those short sharp sessions were proving to be more advantageous to him rather than prolonged periods on the practice pitch where his concentration might falter.
Consequently, his contribution to the Treble-winning team was absolutely immense and I am delighted that he signed for one more season to play in the Champions League.

He remains one of the most gifted footballers I have ever seen or worked with and considering I played with many excellent players at club and international level, I cannot pay him any greater compliment than that.

As good a two-footed player that has played professional football, Lubo Moravcik's own wonderful enthusiasm for this great game remains as keen as ever. His dead-ball kicking is Beckhamesque and his control immaculate.

In only a short period of time at Celtic Park he has become as big a hero as any of the Lisbon Lions of 1967. He must have done something special to have warranted such acclaim.

MARTIN O'NEILL
Celtic manager
October 2001

A LIFE LESS ORDINARY

When he arrived in Glasgow he couldn't speak a word of English. His signing, for £300,000 from German side MSV Duisburg was greeted with a mixture of derision and bemusement; derision that Celtic would spend so little on a 33-year-old, bemusement over the player himself. After all, in the insular word of Scottish football, who had ever heard of Lubomir Moravcik?

Well, there can be no derision or bemusement now, only grateful thanks to Dr Jozef Venglos for having given Celtic fans and Scottish football the opportunity to savour this unique talent.

The boy from the Slovakian village of Mlynarce who was often considered too slight to be picked for youth teams, who would throw tantrums when the older boys wouldn't pass the ball to him, who finally made it as a footballer with his local club, who was sent off at the World Cup, who played in France and was considered by Zinedine Zidane to be one of the best players he ever played against, and who finally arrived under a blaze of negative publicity at Celtic was given a gift – to be able to play football better than most – and we can only be thankful that he was able to share that gift with others.

When 60,000 fans at Celtic Park join as one in chanting "Lubo! Lubo!" it is the ultimate accolade of the ordinary supporters towards a great player who has lived a life less ordinary.

Through the eyes of his Mother Veronika Moravcikova

Many years ago I probably made a mistake. I was twenty when my first son, Robert, was born. Three months after his birth I went back to work and my mother watched the baby.

My second son was born six years later - Lubomir. Being older, I made a different choice, deciding to stay at home and look after the baby, which I did until he was three. Without being really aware of it at that time, I'd started developing our close relationship right from the beginning. Initially, I had wanted a daughter, as did the whole family since we already had a boy, but I was never disappointed. Lubo made it up for me many times over and I would never have swapped him, not even for ten baby girls!

I have two great sons and can rely on both of them. Robert lives in Nitra, and with him being close by, he is always ready to give me a hand with anything. He's quiet, level-headed, and a bit introverted. Lubo is completely different. He can make friends easily and win them over. He is also the type of person who won't bore you for even a minute. With him there's always excitement; there's always something's going on.

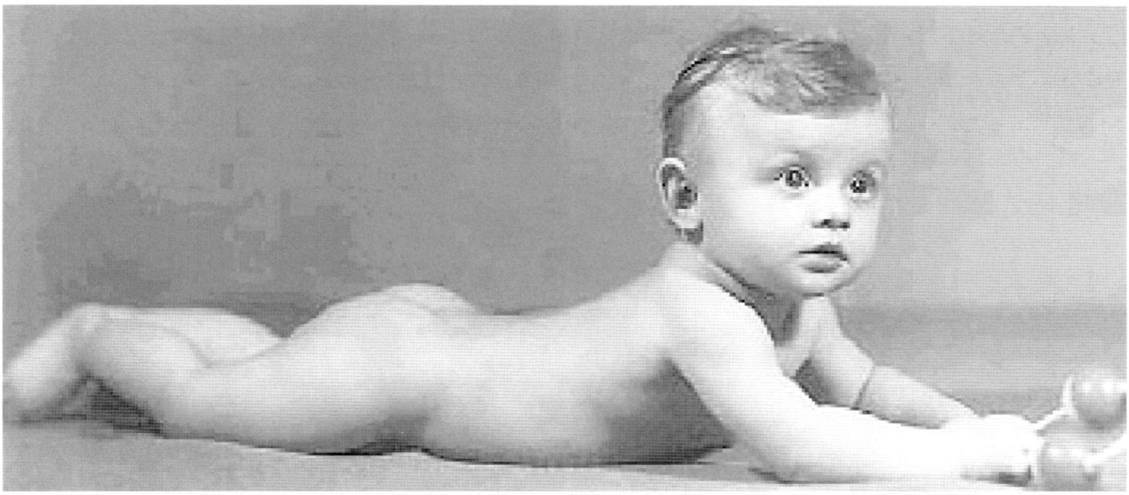

It's as if Robert and Lubomir aren't brothers. They love and understand one another but they have completely different personalities. Lubo, with his spontaneity and directness, took after his father. Robert is more rational, thoughtful and adaptable; he takes more after me. That doesn't mean I get along better with Robert. I just have a soft spot for Lubo, just as I've always had for his father. He's precious to me, mainly because I can never spend enough time with him. When he comes home, everything just revolves around him. Lubo is our family silver.

Ever since they were small I could see differences between my two sons, in just about everything. Lubo wasn't yet 18, didn't have a driving licence but he would still drive a car whenever he could. Robert had to be pushed into take his driving lessons. Then again, Robert can do or make anything with his hands. Lubo is hopeless with his hands; he'd rather hire someone to do it.

But both of them inherited football genes. Robert used to play football as well but, unlike his brother, he wasn't pushy and ambitious enough. He was also a bit sickly, so we didn't let him do everything, but many people agreed that Robert was an even better football talent than Lubo. He didn't have Lubo's determination and conviction, though.

I was taking dancing lessons myself at the time and I'm sure that Lubo could have become a good dancer if he hadn't become a footballer because he has a gift for co-ordinating his movements. He used be to a good ice hockey player and quite a good skier too.

Even when he was an adolescent, Lubo often surprised me with how self-critical he was. If he couldn't do something, he'd try everything to change it. He wouldn't moan, wouldn't be defeated, he would just work on himself, but he could also be quick-tempered and impulsive. Robert would never kick his football boot high up into the sky and keep getting red cards. Even as a boy Lubo could never stand injustice. If he was punished and knew what it was for, he'd be quiet, but if he felt the punishment was unjust, that he was innocent, such as those times when I'd vent my frustrations out on him for no good reason, he'd demand an explanation.

He always worried that he was too slightly built, too small. After he was admitted to the secondary industrial school and went to the class for the first time, the school janitor at the gate directed him to the primary school next door. As a secondary school student, if he went to a disco, he was always asked to show his identity card. He kept saying he feared that he wouldn’t grow much more. In the club or on a football field he'd often be passed over, which made him unhappy.

His father would push him hard although he didn't really have to. Lubo was always a professional, even as a boy. He showed initiative but always knew what his duties were, in school or on the football ground. He always wanted to do everything properly. If he got a bad mark in school, he'd be angry, but not because we gave him into trouble. He just worried and did all he could to improve it.

He was always kicking his ball around but he did his share of work at home. We were always busy in our vineyard and his father would never have tolerated it if Lubo didn't do his share of the work there, but Lubo always listened to his father, respected him and took advice from him. He often also took advice from his Uncle Ed – his father's brother - who, by the way, also used to be a footballer, like Lubo’s dad was.

Lubo spent every spare moment kicking the ball. He and other boys played football everywhere, even in our courtyard where, for years, we tried to grow a lawn but we never succeeded. It would never

grow nice and green, not until Lubo left home.
He went off into the big world of football, became well-known, popular and made money, but the fame never went to his head, and money has not changed him either. He is who he is, with his good qualities and little blemishes, without which it wouldn't be him. He is still the same – amiable - not forgetting his friends, and our relationship has also remained the same. He is considerate and it is mainly because of him that we live very well, without financial problems. He supports the whole family, without any expectation; he does it as a matter of course.

With my husband I went to see almost every match that Lubo played, not just in Nitra, but at many football grounds in Czechoslovakia and especially when he played for the national team. I also saw him playing in France, with St. Etienne and Bastia, and in Glasgow, with Celtic. Mostly they were great occasions, which made me proud, but there were times when a shiver ran down my spine, like at the match in Bastia against Monaco, when Lubo broke his leg. Sitting in the stands I could hear the cracking noise and his painful cry. No mother can go through the moments like that.

However, there are times when I do feel sad. In the past 12 years, there have been many happy meetings but also some sad partings. Lubo flies in, makes the colours of reality brighter, and then off he goes again. I take it hard when he's leaving, and it's getting harder every time. I'm so sad to see him packing to go, especially since my husband died.

Veronika Moravcikova, 62, brought up two sons, matriculated at a secondary school of economics and worked as a clerk. She is now retired.

FIRST TOUCHES

As far as Lubo can remember, football was always the main topic of conversation at home in Mlynarce. The family lived close to the football ground. Jan, his father, played for the local second division side AC Nitra, who won promotion to Czechoslovakia's top league in 1959 for the first time in the club's history.

Lubo loved the endless football chat at home. His dad and his Uncle Ed had debates, discussions and disagreements long into the night, dragging up football stories as they sipped wine from their Sudol vineyard. Lubo could listen to the stories over and over, hanging on to every word the adults said. Soon he knew all their stories and would correct them whenever they were wrong; it was always difficult to get him to go to bed, even when the time had dragged on to near midnight.

Lubo didn't have many friends his own age living in the neighbourhood, but his brother Robert - six years older - often used to bring his friends and they, with little Lubo among them, played football or even ice hockey. The older boys just let him play to make up the numbers, but when they wouldn't pass the ball to him, Lubo often threw a tantrum, rolling around on the ground and kicking his legs in the air because he wanted to have the ball all to himself. He couldn't get enough of the ball and used to practice in a meadow near the house or in the yard of the old disused Bana brickworks until darkness forced him to go home. By that time he would be so tired that he could hardly walk.

He never had other toys and he didn't like to sit at home watching television. For Christmas he always got books about football as presents. It became a tradition in the family so that it became impossible to imagine Christmas without it. Whether he got a football yearbook or a book about some football championship, he read them from cover to cover in just a few days.

Quite often his mother would find him asleep in bed still with his football boots on. Every spare moment was spent practising his skills with a tennis ball. The big football he kept for kicking against the fence and his father, who had to keep repairing it, was forever scolding him for it. Without really realising it at the time, he was going through the best natural and comprehensive football training every day. With his natural athletic talent Lubo did other sports. He was drawn, especially, to ice hockey and despite not being tall, he could hold his own in volleyball or basketball.

It was, however, obvious from the beginning that football would claim him. He was a born footballer. His main advantage was his talent, but besides his talent, to achieve what he wanted he also had to bring in his ability to work hard, his tenacity and his ambition.

To a small boy from Mlynarce, more a village than a suburb of a town, the Nitra football stadium seemed very far away, but Lubo's father was not one who would take his son by the hand and bring him to the club. He spent his time with the family and on his vineyard where he had to work hard. From over seven hundred vines, he was making two thousand litres of wine every year. He did not seem to be concerned with his son's future football career, preferring instead to give it a free rein.

"Go there yourself," he would tell Lubo. "Tell them your name. They'll know who you are."

Lubo could not bring himself to do it. Instead, he joined the team of "little Benjamins" which was the nickname for the boys in the football nursery in Mlynarce. Soon, the team of "little Benjamins" from Mlynarce football nursery got a chance to play against a side from the football nursery of a big club – Plastika Nitra.

This was the first time that Lubo played in a real football match. While his team lost the match 3-2, this was a great encouragement to his fledging football career, and even the result was not too disheartening; the village had shown they could compete with the town. Two weeks later a friend of Lubo, who played for the Plastika nursery team, came to see him in school. "Father Laci says you should come to the training," the boy told Lubo.

Ladislav (Laci) Balaz was the father figure of football in Nitra. A local legend, Balaz used to coach Lubo's father and later on he concentrated on coaching Nitra's youngsters. Even as a schoolboy, Lubo thought his invitation to be an honour and was proud that it was Balaz himself who called him up.

Lubo was at least a year younger than most of the boys in his first Nitra football team. It was a frustrating time for the youngster, and his age dictated that he spent most of the time at the club on the bench. He was annoyed and soon went back to Mlynarce. It was around this time that the Janko Kral School organised a tournament to select boys for its football team. Lubo's cousin and several of his friends already attended the school, so Lubo put his name in for the tournament. He got into the team and while they only played friendly matches against other schools, it gave Lubo the opportunity to train regularly under coach Frantisek Raus and teacher Julius Uvacek.

When he was eleven, towards the end of term, the school organised another football tournament, and the coaches from Plastika Nitra were there to select players for both of their boys' teams. Lubo played well in the tournament, his performances catching the eye of coach Emil Bruchter, who picked him for Plastika Nitra's first team.

As before, Lubo was again at least a year younger than the other boys but this time he played regularly. His best friend, Peter Hnilica, played in the team; some years later they also became related when Peter married Lubo's cousin, Jana.

When, later on, Lubo's friends from the second team joined the first team, it was the beginning of a strong generation of players who eventually brought success to Nitra. In 1979 Lubo's team won the Western Slovak schoolboys' championship, and they followed this with a second-place finish at the Slovak schoolboys' championship in Jelsava. Lubo's team-mates were Blaho, Hnilica, Kollar and Urban, and the youngsters continued playing in the same team until the end of their junior years.

This was a crucial period in Lubo's football career - when he began to develop as a genuine two-footed player, even though he was originally a natural right-footer. With two right-wingers in the team, the coach told Lubo to play on the left because he had more experience, and this is where he stayed, continuing to refine his left foot in training and in games. By the time he made it as a footballer, Lubo was a completely two-footed player.

However, it was not all plain-sailing and the young Lubo's attitude almost saw him walk away from the game before he had even began. At the age of 14, Lubo graduated from the schoolboys' team to the third grade junior team, who competed against sides from other villages in the area. His continued progress and development as a footballer meant that Lubo was still playing against boys who were three and four years older than he was; the fact that Lubo always relied more on skill rather than strength appeared to work against him.

He hardly ever played a game, and more often than not did not even make it on to the bench. After several months he had had enough. He stopped going to training and returned to Mlynarce, trained with the local juniors and sometimes, illegally, without registration, he played for their team, but this situation did not make him any happier. After thinking it over for a while, Lubo decided to give it one last go at Plastika, as much as for the friends he had left behind as for himself. It was to be an important decision.

In the middle of September 1979, he approached coach Stefan Havlicek, who was only too delighted to welcome the young player back into the fold. Soon enough, Lubo was given his chance in several games and ended up playing in the autumn season. In the last game of the season he was named man-of-the-match.

If his own determination not to give up had a bearing on how his career subsequently turned out, then a reorganisation of youth football in the area was also to have a profound influence on Lubo's career. A new Under-16 age category was set up, with Plastika forming a team to compete at that level, and Lubo became a star. Coached by the former player Frantisek Halas, Lubo was able to establish himself regularly in the team and was now playing against boys his own age and physique. Soon his exploits were attracting interest from elsewhere in the Plastika club.

Lubo quickly graduated straight to the first grade junior team, courtesy of coach Otto Kanas, but while Lubo would more often than not be part of the starting 11, he rarely finished a game. He was second to none in terms of skill and playing ability but he still lacked the physical strength of his team-mates or opponents.

THE LEAGUE FOOTBALLER

He always wanted to wear number ten, like Michel Platini or Diego Maradona, but instead got stuck with number six - like his father.

Lubo pulled on his junior league football boots for the first time in a competitive match against Puchov. His debut indicated that this was not just another ordinary player coming through. One newspaper report on the game seemed to indicate that the reporter had spotted something special on the pitch. The report read: "The star of Nitra team was tiny Moravcik. We are certainly going to hear from him in the future." Lubo's classmates put the newspaper clipping of this prophetic comment up on the school board, and he still has this clipping in his archive. It was the first public notice to announce the appearance of a new football star, but it was going to take some time before this star would be at its brightest. The road to the top was to be long and winding but he wasn't going to get lost on it.

In his last junior season he was the key player in the team. His coach was Milan Lesicky, a man who was to follow Lubo's career for quite some time. Lesicky became coach of the senior Nitra team playing in the Czechoslovak first division, achieving the remarkable feat of getting Nitra into the UEFA Cup. Later he became joint manager of the last Czechoslovak national side before the break-up of the country, alongside Milan Macala.

Lubo was now an old head in the junior team, ready to play his last year at this level, and as younger players came into the side, Lubo was certain his place in the team was assured. He was in for a shock. During the first game, a friendly, Lesicky substituted him and then kept him on the bench for the next game. The decision puzzled and angered Lubo but when he was restored to the team for the start of the season, scoring the winning goal in the process, his coach's motives became clear. It was Lesicky's way of telling Lubo to keep his feet on the ground. The young star had become big-headed, thinking there was no-one better than him. The coach had noticed this arrogance creeping into Lubo's attitude and immediately let him know that if he wanted to be in the team, if he wanted to play, then he had to remain competitive and keep fighting for his place.

This was the end of junior football for one generation. There were more new players now coming into the team - Lubo's peers from the nursery and schoolboy teams - and the new coach of the junior team was now Stefan Havlicek, previously Lesicky's assistant. In his last junior season, Lubo helped his team win the 1982 Slovak Junior Championship and come second in the Czechoslovak Federal Championship after losing in the final to Brno. This was a clear signal that Nitra had a good base of young players and that the policy of concentrating on youngsters was now paying dividends.

Lubo's slight build was to cause problems in the coming years, though. This was probably the reason why he was never selected for any junior national sides - the coaches were taking notice of other players. Looking back, Milan Lesicky still does not see this to have been a great tragedy for Lubo.

"It's hard to say what is best for an exceptionally talented player," explained Lesicky. "And in Lubo's case I stress the word 'exceptional'. Maybe it was, in a way, fortunate that Lubo's entry into big-time football was somewhat complicated. Talented players usually skip the age categories, normally playing in higher grades while they are still juniors. The result is an excessive stress on their physical constitution which can lead to frequent injuries and young players may also lose their motivation to develop their talent to the best of their capabilities.

"Lubo's development as a player in this respect was different, untypical. Because of his slight build he kept playing football in his own age category. The fact is, though, that in junior teams' leagues, points already become a high priority. This brings pressure on many coaches who then prefer physically stronger rather than skilful players, which, I think, is simply wrong. In my time in Nitra coaching youngsters, from 1982 until summer 1988, we could never really get rid of this pressure."

It was not until the very end of his last junior season that Pavel Krsek selected Lubo in the Slovak junior team which was to go on a tour abroad, but even this wasn't without difficulties. There was supposed to be just one player in the squad from each club, but in the end Milan Lesicky got his way, insisting that two players from Nitra team - Hnilica and Moravcik - should travel.

Lubo was disappointed that he didn't get into one of the federal selections. Only Lubo Kollar made it into the Czechoslovak Federal junior team from Nitra. It was generally accepted that it was easier for players from bigger clubs like Slovan Bratislava, Sparta Prague or Banik Ostrava to get selected for Czechoslovakia. These clubs had a long-established reputation for their successful youth policies and Nitra, in this respect, were just starting out.

After his excellent final season with the junior side, in which Lubo became one of the best players, it was time for the big decision by the club – who would be selected for the senior team. It was apparent that only three junior players were going to be promoted. After the last training session, Milan Lesicky came into the dressing room and read out the three names - Peter Hnilica, Brano Varga and Tibor Urban.

Lubo was stunned. He had been absolutely certain that he would have been one of the three. He had no objection again Hnilica - he was the captain and one of the best players. His selection made perfect sense. The other two were certainly very good players but their contribution to the overall team performance was not as significant as that of Hnilica and Moravcik.

Lubo was convinced that attacking, creative players had a more important role than defenders. He thought the reason for his omission was again due to his slight build. It was difficult to take because, to his mind, the concerns regarding physical strength were groundless. Previously, there had been regular physical tests that all players had to take and certain criteria they had to meet before they could be included in the senior squad. Lubo passed these tests without any problem. This only confirmed his opinion that, in terms of physical strength, he was up to it. The tests usually ended with five 300-metre sprints, which really tested the stamina.

However, during games Lubo was able to compliment physical strength with the qualities that made him stand out among the others: ability to play with either foot, brilliant ball skills, ability to read the play and the general ability to play and entertain at the same time. He was also noted for his courage in tackling; he could give it just as good as he could take it.

Milan Lesicky, who was then Lubo's coach, always dismissed the opinions that suggested Lubo lacked sufficient stamina and strength. He was working with him in the winter and summer preseason periods and could confirm that Lubo, in any respect, was never left behind by his physically stronger team-mates. Lubo was able to pace himself throughout the entire match. He was fast and quick off the mark to be able to use his ball skills, especially his dribbling ability.

Lubo believed that he should have been joining the others in the senior squad for the spring season, and he considered his omission unfair, but displaying characteristic determination, he vowed to show the club officials that they had been wrong in their selection.

Through the eyes of coach Stefan Havlicek

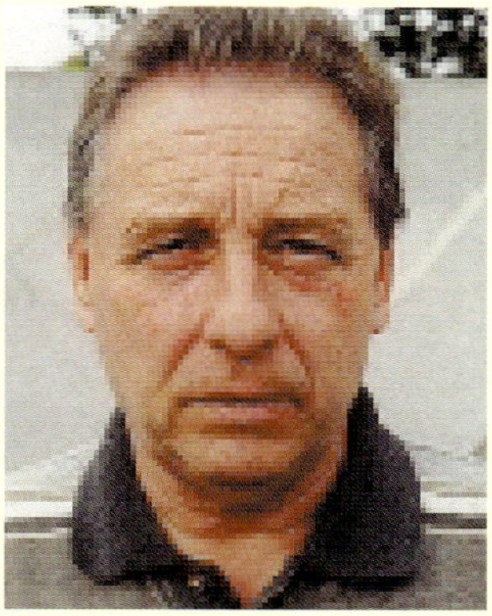

"Come on, pack it up, leave it for tomorrow – I had to shout quite often to get him off the pitch. It was getting dark and the groundsman wanted to go home. He just went to bed and got up with the football."

I've followed Lubo's football career right from the beginning in Nitra. I saw his gradual development from the schoolboys to the junior team that won the 1982 Slovak Junior Championship. I was with this team as an assistant to Milan Lesicky.

For a long time Lubo kept his small-boy's look on and off the pitch. This was due mainly to his size. He always took his football very seriously but with boyish sincerity and spontaneity. He was a lovely boy. Even though some of his peers were taller and stronger, at training, everyone always wanted to be in the same team as him. Even as a boy, Lubo stood out among the others, especially because of his will to win, always leading by example. Even at that age he was a natural leader. He was ambitious too, in a good sense. He could get angry too when he was losing, sometimes he would throw himself on the ground in frustration. But these were just the tantrums that go with being young.

I remember an episode which shows how emotional he was about his football right from the beginning. When he was still in the nursery team we were invited to an indoor tournament in Trebisov, which was organised for the week between Christmas and New Year. We took the team there in three cars. Lubo played really well. On a smaller pitch his exceptional ball skills could show up even more. We won the tournament but he scored only one goal and even that was disallowed although there was nothing wrong with the goal. After that he was frustrated and very unhappy for a long time.

I also remember one match when Lubo was thirteen, playing for the second schoolboys' team. As in every game, he was dribbling with the ball, going past the opposition players – but this time he did that when the score was 1–0, with a few minutes to go and just outside the penalty box. The game was played on a poor cinder pitch and he lost the ball and the opposition equalised. Afterwards I didn't make much out of it; in the dressing room I just quietly told him that this is not done in football. He sat in the dressing room for a long time, head in his hands, and after that he didn't turn up for training for the next two weeks. That's how hard he took it. Of course, he got over it and two weeks later came to the dressing room and asked me to take him back. Lubo could disarm people with his sincerity and directness. No-one could stay angry with him for too long, but even as he grew up, his actions or responses are never caused by bad or malicious intentions.

Once more he came to me asking me to take him back. That was in 1979. By this time he was in the third grade juniors, with boys three or four years older than him. Because of his build he couldn't quite compete with them and was often on the bench. After a while he decided that he didn't like that, and he stopped coming to the training sessions but it didn't take long before he was back. By then he had friends in the team and they were, I think, the main reason that Lubo reconsidered his decision.

Soon things started to go better for him, he settled down in the team and started to play on regular basis and from then on he just started improving and got better and better. To a coach he was a great player to work with, despite his occasional outbursts, because his optimistic and positive approach to everything he did always took over. If he got angry it was only for a short time - like a black cloud covering the sun but five minutes later it's bright again.

He was already aware that he had talent. He could see that he was better than most of the boys but he would never show that. What's more, unlike many others, he was prepared to work hard to develop his talent. Quite often he'd stay on the pitch for extra training, on his own or with some of his team-mates. "Come on, pack it up, leave it for tomorrow," I had to shout quite often to get him off the pitch. It was getting dark and the groundsman wanted to go home. He just went to bed and got up with the football.

He was dexterous, fast, and he was always good on the ball. All of us who worked with him in Nitra always knew that he'd go far if he persevered. I'm glad to see that I wasn't wrong. He can still appreciate that at the Nitra stadium he received a good grounding that stood him in good stead for professional football. He doesn't have to be reminded that if it weren't for all those who helped him here in Nitra, he wouldn't get that far, he himself says so quite often. Whenever he comes home he never fails to call at the stadium. He comes to see me quite often too, asking what's new, what I'm doing and talking football, and he is the same with others, he didn't get a big head and his personality, I'd say, is still the same. He didn't change. He's able to talk football for hours. I'm convinced he'll stay in football even after he finishes playing. He'll be able to use his great experience. He's also a good organiser and I can see he'd be able to keep together and direct a strong team of people interested in football.

Stefan Havlicek, 55, spent over twenty years coaching young players in Nitra. He then became a full-time club official. At present he is a Secretary for Youth Development in the Slovak Football Association.

RETURN HOME

The question now facing Lubo was a simple one, yet of vital importance to his future. What next? Thankfully, he had only 24 hours after his rejection by Nitra to contemplate it before a call came from Vrable offering to take him on loan. It meant a step down to the Slovakian second division, but with the rules stating that every team had to have at least two players under the age of 20 in their squad, with one required to be selected to play in the team, Lubo stood a good chance of getting a regular game.

Joining Vrable, he found himself in an experienced team, some of whom he knew from Nitra. More importantly, the coach Edo Borovsky gave him a chance in the team, which Lubo seized upon, playing regularly and impressing everyone with his performances.

Throughout this time, he was still attending the secondary industrial school, with his final leaving exams looming in the spring, and having got over the disappointment of being overlooked by Nitra, Lubo began to see the positive aspects of his move to Vrable. He was getting a regular game in a less demanding league, and he was also able to devote more time to his schoolwork. Vrable, in effect, had thrown him a lifeline.

It was also a time when Lubo began to improve the physical side of his game. His slight build had always appeared to hinder his progress, particularly at Nitra but now, between the ages of 18–19, he grew bigger and stronger, and with this physical maturity his best qualities as footballer – his football brain, his touch and technique - developed even further.

Even though Nitra had not promoted Lubo to the senior squad, his progress at Vrable was still being monitored by the club, who were going through a sticky patch under coach Frantisek Urvay, and a friendly between Nitra and Vrable proved an excellent opportunity for the young Moravcik to impress the Nitra management team. He seized the opportunity with both feet and it wasn't long before he reaped the rewards.

With increasing demands from his school work, Lubo was often forced to miss training with Vrable, opting instead to train with the junior team in Nitra. One night, after training, a Nitra official approached Lubo. The young player was ordered to report the following day for a friendly match against Chrenova. It was unexpected but Lubo didn't hesitate. Nitra beat Chrenova 13–0, with Lubo playing the entire second half.

After the game, he was told to report for training with Nitra the following day. Lubo's stint with Vrable was at an end after just 10 games. By the end of the same week he was with the Nitra first team, preparing for a league match against Teplice. At the pre-match camp, the coach announced the starting line-up the day before the game, stating that Lubo was to play as the left winger. Moravcik made no response to the news. He presumed that the coach was referring to Lubo Kollar, who was sitting next to him.

After a while Moravcik turned to Kollar: "Well, how do you feel before the match?" he asked. Kollar looked at him surprised: "What do you mean? It's you who's playing, not me."

It was an emotional moment for Moravcik and he had to compose himself as tears welled up in his eyes. What has been his dream was now on the verge of becoming a reality. On October 16, 1983, Lubomir Moravick realised one of his football dreams - he played a first team game for Nitra.

If the date is still etched in his mind, memories of the game are a little hazier for Lubo now. It was late autumn, and the game was one of the last to be played before the winter break. He had one shot on goal and twice he got past the Teplice defenders, but Nitra did not win. The match ended in a draw, and it also heralded the end for coach Urvay, who was replaced by Lopata. For the rest of the autumn season Moravcik remained in the squad, and made two further appearances, against Vitkovice and Bohemians Prague.

With his football career still in its infancy, with no clear indication that it would grow to full maturity, Lubo was confronted by a conflict between football and education. The Nitra team was getting ready for winter training but it clashed with Lubo's leaving exams in the coming spring. His father then stepped in, declaring that Lubo's main priority was to finish school. So for a second time, Lubo went on loan, this time to Sala. It was exactly the same story as Vrable. After 10 games for Sala, Lubo returned to Nitra, to a club that had just been relegated. The only good news for Lubo came off the field, where he passed his leaving exams.

This, however, presented problems for Lubo, in that he now had to decide what he wanted to do. He could do his military service now, playing in an army team and he did consider this option. Most of friends in football were going to be conscripted and he hoped he could get into the same team with Peter Hnilica. His father was of a different opinion, advising him to go to university. That will be your foundation for life, not football, his father told him. Lubo evidently took his dad's advice and passed the admission exams to University of Agriculture, Faculty of Agronomy, to specialise in Land Improvement and Irrigation. Despite this, he wasn't admitted because of the shortage of places. He appealed against the decision and, on a second attempt, he was accepted.

Lubo would later say that this is what saved his football career. He remained in the same environment, lived with his parents and kept playing for Nitra, who, despite being relegated to the second division, were laying the foundations for a good future, thanks in no small part to the crop of youngsters coming through the ranks. Lubo was a leading light in this group.

Nitra didn't manage to return to the top flight as quickly as they hoped, the club finishing runners-up to DAC Dunajska Streda. The season was a valuable one for Nitra's youngsters, with the team sometimes fielding as many as six players under the age of 20. The experience gained at this time would prove beneficial but in the short term, it was the more experienced Dunajska Streda who won promotion to the first division.

Nitra then took the decision to bring in a new coach, Jozef Jarabinsky replacing Stanislav Jarabek. Jarabinsky realised the benefits of bringing in young players but was more successful in blending them in with the experienced players at the club. The two Lubos – Moravcik and Koller – were now regulars in the side and there was already another strong generation of youngsters – Lednicky, Mikus, Halas, Ondruska, awaiting their chance behind them. The next season Nitra started strongly and by the halfway stage were top of the table after beating Slovan Bratislava 3-1 at home. Everything seemed to be going well, for Nitra and for Moravcik, but further difficulties were just around the corner. During the winter break, Plastika Nitra travelled to Siofok in Hungary for a friendly game. The match was played on a difficult, icy pitch, which cost Lubo dearly. He twisted his ankle and was out of action for two weeks. When the season re-started he found himself on the bench again. Later he described this period as critical in his football career.

FATHER STEPS IN

This was to be the first but also the last time that his father had a significant effect on Lubo's football career. Until then Jan Moravcik's main worry was for his son to do well in school. Football to him was a secondary matter. His attitude was – if you're good enough, you'll make it, if not, no-one will be able to help you. This time, however, he openly broke his principle.

Jan Moravcik had a meeting with Nitra club officials and gave them an ultimatum. "My son has to start playing, otherwise he'll go to Zilina." The secretary of Zilina was Anton Krasnohorsky, a good friend of Jan Moravcik's. Lubo's other transfer, to Zilina's University of Transportation, had already been worked out too. The intervention came just in time. Nitra realised that they could not afford to lose a talent like Lubo, so he was restored to the first team, at the expense of Karol Herak.
Back in the team, Lubo played in all Nitra's remaining matches, helping them clinch promotion to the first division. It was a time of celebration, at the club and in the town, but it also signalled the end for Jarabinsky, who resigned as coach, to be replaced by Kamil Majernik.

By now Lubo had played over 50 games for Nitra. He played on the left side of midfield, having taken over from Rudo Kramolis, who was transferred to Inter Bratislava, with Zolo Molnar on the right and Robo Jez in the middle. The other key players in the Nitra side were the experienced Kamil Chatrnuch and Dusan Borko. The greatest challenge still faced Lubo and his team-mates. They had triumphed in the second division but would they be able to cope with the demands of the top league? Lubo was now 20 and eagerly looked forward to it.

Nitra's return to the first division was painful, to say the least. Their first game, an away match in Ostrava, saw the newly-promoted side lose 5-1, while their opening game at home, against Bohemians, resulted in a 3-2 defeat. This defeat, however, also proved to be a milestone in Lubo's career – his first goal in Czechoslovakia's top league. The goal, a shot from outside the penalty box in the last minute of the match, only reduced the margin of Nitra's defeat, but it is one Lubo can still recall to this day. It also reassured him of his ability, and from then on he knew he could score goals at this level. In the following weeks results gradually improved for Nitra and they found themselves in the unusual position of being middle of the table. Nitra's supporters were used to the team fighting to avoid relegation. They were enjoying the new experience and the heady heights of mid-stable security.

Lubo was playing his part in the team's success but he was also about to take another step forward in his own career. As the season resumed after the winter break, Lubo received a letter inviting him to join the Czechoslovakian Olympic football team for a match in Switzerland. In the mid 1980s, it was virtually Czechoslovakia's second national team. Lubo found himself joining up with a squad that included players like Kubik, Knoflicek and Chovanec – all regulars in Czechoslovakia's national side.

The trip was a great experience for the young Nitra player, further boosted by the fact he came on as a substitute for the last 10 minutes of the game. It was the first time he had ever wore the shirt of the national team. Even though this was only the Olympic squad, it was still difficult to get into the team. There were some excellent players in the squad, people like Petr Herda or Jan Kocian, and Lubo was a novice among them. It's important not to underestimate the giant leap Lubo had made in terms of Czechoslovakian football; a player who had never been selected to represent his country at any level, not even for the junior national team, was now in the Olympic squad. People in the game began to sit and take notice of Lubomir Moravcik.

His impressive form for Nitra confirmed that his selection for the Olympic squad had not been a mistake, and he was called up again, this time for a match in the German Democratic Republic (the former East Germany). This time Lubo played for the last 20 minutes of the game.

Before his call-up, the Olympic team had already played one game

in their qualification group for the 1988 Seoul Olympics, losing 2-0 against Austria. The defeat forced the coach, Milos Kvacek to look for new players and Moravcik was one of them. The next game was against Finland in Dunajska Streda. This time, Lubo was selected to play from the start, on the left wing, and Czechoslovakia triumphed 2-0. More importantly for Lubo, he scored one of the goals. The qualification campaign continued successfully, apart from one disastrous result – a 1-0 defeat in Kuwait. Finally, it all came down to one match, an away game in Yugoslavia. A draw would be enough to send the Czechs to the Olympics, but in the end, they lost 1-0 to a Yugoslav side full of outstanding players who would go on to be become top stars, like Savicevic, Katanec and Stojkovic.

Altogether, Lubo played 11 games for the Olympic team. It was a valuable experience for him, increasing his motivation and confidence, and this was mirrored in his performances for Nitra, where he was now a key player. The next step, logically, was his selection for the Czechoslovakian national team. His boyhood dreams were, one by one, becoming a reality. He had only one wish: not to stumble and fall at the next hurdle.

Through the eyes of his Uncle Eduard Moravcik

"At least five times he broke the fence kicking the football against it. His father used to be very annoyed and shouted at him, but I think he was also saying to himself: "Maybe he'll get somewhere one day."

When Lubo was starting to play senior football, he went on loan to Sala, and during that short time they played in the Slovakian Cup against Trnava, who were coached by the famous Anton Malatinsky. I was at the match with my brother, Lubo's father. We were standing near Trnava's bench and Malatinsky was up near the byline, shouting directions to his players. Right in front of him Lubo dribbled past two Trnava players and crossed the ball. He did it again a moment later. Malatinsky turned to his bench and shouted: "Who's that little bugger?"

My brother Jano was quick to call to Malatinsky: "That's my son!" Malatinsky looked at him for a while before asking: "And who are you?" Jano replied that his name was Moravcik, that he used to play against him for Nitra and that he might remember him. Malatinsky did. "Yes, I remember, but that's a handy player, that boy of yours. I'd take him anytime," he said. Jano then put on a bit of a show, just to stir the Nitra officials who were standing near-by watching the game, and sure enough, they soon started shouting: "He's a Nitra player. No one's going to take him."

We all could see that Lubo was a great talent, ever since he was small. His father and I were convinced that it was only going to be a matter of time before he would make it. Most of his friends were older than him and this made him look even smaller than he was, but in the game he would make up for it with his nimbleness; he was dexterous, fast, quick off the mark.

He spent a lot of time on the substitutes' bench. It was obvious that he was good enough but he wasn't yet strong enough. It was only when he came into the junior team that Milan Lesicky started to push him, and then gave him a chance, which Lubo took.

With my brother I probably saw every game Lubo played, right from when he began with the nursery team. Often we'd sit at my brother's place talking football till late. We both used to play football so it was our favourite subject. Lubo would sit next to us, listening to every word. He knew all of our stories backwards and when we would forget something while telling them again, Lubo was quick to correct us. His father had a hard job trying to get him to bed before midnight. Lubo wouldn't go to bed for the world.

When he was fourteen, maybe fifteen, he got angry with his father who, in a joke, was goading him in front of me: "You're never going to be a good footballer". I remember Lubo, standing there with tears

in his eyes, full of the boyish insolence, telling his father: "Just you wait. I will play for the national team." He was always ambitious. He still is.
At least five times he broke the fence at home kicking the football against it. His father used to be very annoyed and shouted at him, but I think he was also saying to himself: "Maybe he'll make it one day." He kept telling Lubo that school had to come first, but he closely watched Lubo's development as footballer and was proud of him. Once he told me that he'd be really happy if Lubo could become a good player. He was even willing to accept that Lubo might not finish his schooling.

In fact, his son's football came first for Lubo's father. I think I can say that now, but he'd never tell that to his son. He hoped that Lubo could get further than he himself did. Jano finished high school, so Lubo must finish university; he was a second division footballer, Lubo must play in the first division. He was really hard on him. He kept telling Lubo: "If you want to study and play football at the same time, you'll be home by nine every day!" And Lubo did that without fail most of the time. Five minutes past nine, and his father would be out looking for him; quarter past nine, and there would be hell to pay. It was like that even when Lubo started university, right up until he got married.

I remember once, Lubo's father and I wanted to pull some strings for him at the university. Lubo was playing for the Czechoslovakian Olympic team so he missed a few weeks' lectures. One of the professors said he wouldn't let him sit the exam at the end of the year. We knew the university's secretary of the Communist Party and were set to go and see him. Lubo found out about it and told his father that if we did, he'd never go to university ever again. He said he didn't want anyone to sort out the exams for him like that; he'd pass the exams without any help from anyone. In the end, he had to repeat the year but eventually he graduated.

Only once did his father do something which had an effect on Lubo's football career. Nitra were in the second division at the time, and were coached by Jozef Jarabinsky. Lubo sprained his ankle and, even after he was fit again, he couldn't get back into the team although he had been a regular before and was playing well before his injury. Tono Krasnohorsky, a family friend, was at that time manager of Zilina, who played in the first division. So Lubo's father offered his son to Zilina. The club were prepared to take him, and Krasnohorsky even sent a letter confirming that Zilina were interested in Lubo, whereupon Jano went to see Nitra's coach and told Jarabinsky that if Lubo remained on the bench, he was off to Zilina. Soon Lubo was playing again and eventually became a fixture in the starting line-up.

At that time Nitra had a good bunch of players who stuck together. There were some big names among them too: Robo Jez, Peter Paluch, Kamil Chatrnuch, Zolo Molnar, Fero Halas, Milan Lednicky. Once a month the whole team met at the Moravcik house for a glass of wine. Lubo's mother would prepare some food and the team sat there talking football. No-one ever drank more than one or two glasses of wine. Plastika Nitra were still in the second division and were coached by Stano Jarabek, and he always turned up around nine to see what was going on and take his team home.

Some of the talk, especially about football, was quite sharp at those meetings. For quite some time, Lubo's father and I couldn't accept Robo Jez, who had come to Nitra from Bratislava. He was a young and talented player but somehow we couldn't take to him. He was unconvincing, we thought, but Lubo was always defending him. You don't understand, he told his father on one occasion. Soon enough, Robo showed us what a good footballer he was, he really pulled the Nitra team along. Lubo's judgment concerning his ability was spot on.

After Czechoslovakia qualified for the 1990 World Cup in Italy, Lubo received 80,000 crowns. He came home, put the money on the table and told his father: "Buy yourself a new car with this."

Jano bought himself a brand new Skoda Favorit. After he died, Lubo gave the car to me. I still have it, it goes well and I can tell everyone that I'm driving a car from the World Cup. Lubo was, and is, very generous. For the Mlynarce football club, where he started as a boy, he bought a set of new strips and he also helps other people without talking about it. When he comes home, the first thing he says to me is – where are we playing on Sunday, uncle? And we're off to the match.

In 1965, the year Lubo was born, the family got new central heating for their house. The installation wasn't quite finished so it didn't work properly. Lubo's father decided he had to do something about it. He put some petrol into it, lit a match and BANG!! - the whole house was full of soot. Little Lubo in his cot was covered all over, black as a chimney-sweep. His mother came in and when she saw the room, she started crying. She was full anger and fear. First she ran to little Lubo. When she saw he was alright, that nothing happened to him, she calmed down. Soot brings luck she said, and added: "He'll certainly get somewhere one day." And she was right.

Uncle Eduard Moravcik, 64, brother of Lubo's father, is a former Nitra player. He used to work as a printer. He is now retired.

NATIONAL PRIDE

Lubo's debut for the Czechoslovakian national team came on 11 November 1987 in Prague, when the home side beat beat Wales 2–0 in a qualification game for the European Championship. However, the result was of more benefit to Denmark, who eventually qualifed from the group for the Euro '88 finals.

The game against Wales also saw Lubo become the first footballer from a Slovak club in the starting line-up of the Czechoslovakia national team since 1983. The last one before then had been Ladislav Jurkemik from Inter Bratislava, who had played against Sweden.

The Czechoslovakian coach was Jozef Venglos, whose path would later cross again with Lubo when player and manager joined up at Celtic.

The 1988/89 season was also to be Lubo's best so far. After two years, Nitra's coach Kamil Majernik was replaced by Milan Lesicky. Under Majernik, Nitra had finished seventh and eighth in the

league, but they were to reach heady heights under Lesicky. At the end of the season, Nitra finished third in the league, qualifying for the UEFA Cup in the process. It was an historic achievement for the club.

Moravcik's performances that season were exceptional and brought about further recognition. He also played several memorable games for Nitra that season, none more so than the 1-0 victory over champions Sparta Prague, when Lubo scored the only goal of the game. A year later Nitra crushed Sparta Prague, who were to win the title again, 4–0. Moravcik dominated the game, also scoring a fantastic solo goal after running nearly the full length of the pitch. He was constantly losing his marker, the Sparta defender Cabala, and put on a little show too. As his injured team-mate Bochnovic was limping off the field, Moravcik picked him up and carried him on the shoulders to the bench, to the enthusiastic applause of the spectators.

Similar stunts were becoming his trademark. In the second leg against FC Cologne in the UEFA Cup, he nutmegged Hassler, the West German internationalist, and he did the same to the Portuguese defender Joao Pinto. To criticisms that he wasted his energy with pointless tricks Lubo's usual reply was: "I want to have fun, to enjoy football, even more so when the game is hard-fought. These tricks actually make me settle down in the game, give me confidence. Who knows, they may affect the opposition's confidence and help to score a goal."

The Nitra side became a well-knitted group of players. At training they would goad one another. Lubo's training partner was usually goalkeeper Peter Paluch. Lubo often played practical jokes on Peter who never failed to return them. In one training match, Lubo was about to take the deciding penalty kick; taking penalties was never one of his strengths. Lubo made a run up to strike the ball when Peter performed a cartwheel, then threw himself up and caught the poorly struck ball as the rest of the players rolled on the ground laughing.

For the first match in the World Cup qualification group against Belgium, Venglos picked a squad of eighteen players. Two of them were to be left out of the team before the game. One of those players was Tomas Skuhravy, later the star of the World Cup in Italy. Moravcik got in but was left on the bench and only came on for the last few minutes of the game. For the next game against Austria, the coach called up Jan Kocian, Lubo's old friend from the Czechoslovakia Olympic team. Lubo was happy for his friend to get a chance in the national team. Later, on international trips, they roomed together. Venglos told both the young Slovakian players that they had a real chance to become regular members of the team he was building. The game in Austria ended in a 2-0 win, with Stano Griga scoring both goals. It was a good start for the Czechoslovakian side, and Kocian and Moravcik, who both started the game, impressed.

Moravcik considers 1989 to be one of the most important years in his football career. Besides playing with Nitra in the UEFA Cup - the greatest achievement in the history of club - he also became a member of the national team which qualified for the 1990 World Cup in Italy. As if this wasn't enough, Lubo was also doing exceptionally well off the pitch and in that year he also graduated from university with an engineering degree – not in June as planned but in December.

That year he was runner-up in the Czechoslovakian Footballer of the Year Award, which was won by Michal Bilek of Sparta Prague. However, when he collected his award, Bilek said: "I've got most of the points in the voting but to me the best player was Lubo Moravcik. He's a universal player, with exceptional ball skills and can also carry a game in great style."

Lubo was also confirming another of his inherent qualities. The better the opposition, the more motivated he became. He was never a leader in the training sessions but he was a big game player. He was at his best in the electrifying atmosphere in front of the huge crowds, facing the best players. This is when he grew in stature.

RED CARD AT THE WORLD CUP

Lubo married Zuzana Stredakova in 1987. Their son Matus was born a year later. It was a difficult time for Lubo, having to divide his time between his family and school, and also between club and international football. At the same time, he discovered that family life had a stabilising effect. With the support of his wife and family; he managed not only to get through this difficult time but thrive on it.

After his graduation, the time came for military service, and it seemed certain that he would be conscripted. It was more or less decided that he would go to the Banska Bystrica army team. The coach there was Jarabek, who had already worked with him at Nitra. "I'll be glad to have you," he told him when they met once by chance.

Ivan Hasek from Sparta Prague was also finishing university at that time. When Lubo spoke to him about his impending military service, Hasek told Moravcik that he had applied to have his military service deferred as it was only a short time before the World Cup in Italy and he didn't want to have his preparation disrupted. Lubo followed his example; he was granted a deferral so he didn't have to turn up for military service until September 1, 1990, after the World Cup in Italy.

But 1990 wasn't as good as the previous year. He experienced some difficulties and at one stage he even considered ending his football career. He clashed with the Nitra coach, Milan Lesicky, who, in Lubo's view, had stopped listening to his players, even to the older, more experienced ones, and didn't talk as openly to them as he had in the previous season. As a result, their working relationship deteriorated. Where before, even if Lubo disagreed with the coach they could talk about it, now there was no communication. Lubo would often say Lesicky used to be a good listener, but he apparently adopted a new, western style of management and the team had to accept it. Still, in a year's time their mutual trust had disappeared.

Lubo disagreed with some of Lesicky's decisions and made the mistake of telling him so in front of the players. Later, Lubo realised that he should have discussed his grievances with the coach in private. At the end of the season they had cleared up the disagreements between them, but it was too late. Nitra's performance in the league wasn't as good as in the previous year.

The team finished sixth, missing out on a UEFA Cup place by just two points. Given the achievements of the previous season this was regarded as a failure for Nitra.

Preparations for the World Cup weren't any smoother. The inclusion of Knoflicek and Kubik, coming from foreign clubs, had an unsettling effect on the team. Lubo was among those who thought that their arrival, so close before the World Cup, wasn't beneficial to the team. It also meant changes to the line-up. Kubik was predominantly a left-footed player, and in the course of the World Cup, Moravcik found himself on the right of the midfield, with Ivan Hasek an attacking right defender just behind him. This was the first and last time in his career that he found himself back on the right, where he had started as a youngster.

However, it was a tactic used to great effect by Venglos, at least until they faced Germany in the quarter-finals. Czechoslovakia lost the match and also lost Moravcik, who was sent off by an Austrian referee for kicking away his own boot which he had lost in a tackle.

Lubo's own harsh conclusions about the tournament were that he hadn't really been ready for the World Cup, either as a person or as a footballer. Until then his career had seemed to be developing gradually, with a real sense of continuity - the juniors, then the third division, then the second, the first, and finally the Olympic team – a logical development. While he was pleased to have played in the World Cup he wanted another crack at it. He knew he still lacked the experience of regular football at the highest international level, which came later in his career. It was not until the age of 28 or 29 that he fully matured as a player.

Unfortunately, he never got a chance to play in another World Cup. In the following years Czechoslovakia failed to qualify for either the World Cup or the European Championship.

The 1990 World Cup ended on a low point for Moravcik and Czechoslovakia, but it had not all been negative. The team had reached the quarter-finals, after all, and Venglos had moulded the players into an effective team unit. It could have been even better, and Lubo had to admit that it was partly his fault that the team didn't get past the quarter-finals because, at a crucial moment in the game against Germany, his country was weakened by his sending-off, but he felt he had the necessary qualities as a footballer, which he would be able to use to greater advantage four years later at another World Cup. Unfortunately, it was not to be.

Still, he enjoyed his time in the national team and, at least until 1990, he was lucky to have played in some really wonderful matches.

Through the eyes of coach Milan Lesicky

"He was, and still is, every inch a footballer."

I think I've spent a longer time than any other coach working with Lubo. He was in my junior team in the 1982–83 season, and then I coached him in the Nitra league team from 1988 until the summer of 1990 when he went to France. After that I had him in the Czechoslovakia national team until April 1993.

I was quite involved in his development as a footballer but I can't say that my contribution to his growth was all that important or crucial. You see, he was simply a born footballer and all that he's achieved is due to his own talent and effort.

I'd like to think that both of us, he as a player and I as a coach, contributed a great chapter to the history of football at Nitra. We won the junior league, we became a top Slovakian team playing in the senior federal competition and we played in the UEFA Cup, which to this day remains Nitra's greatest achievement in football. Until then Plastika Nitra had never provided a key player for the Czechoslovakia national team.

If he hadn't taken up football, Lubo would have been great in some other sport. He was good at ice hockey and he was a good tennis player too. He was a rare, exceptional talent with an incredible will to win, but he had to fight for his spot as a top-level footballer – he was constantly asked to prove himself.

In 1983 a few players from the Nitra juniors were to be selected for the senior team playing in the first division. Lubo wasn't among them. Some officials, ex-players and coaches in the club thought he wasn't physically strong and would only last twenty minutes in a match. He went on loan to Vrable. At that time his father often reproached me for not keeping him at Nitra. My father used to play football with Lubo's father and our families were friends, but he never failed to criticise me, politely but strongly, about that. He was very annoyed about it, and I knew he was right.

I'd tried to convince him that this was the best thing for Lubo. He would play regularly, rather than sitting on the bench. In time I could see that I was right, and Lubo got his chance to play in the senior league team. It was his sincerity and love of football that won through in the end. Later, to the coach of Czechoslovakia Olympic team, Milos Kvacek, he again had to demonstrate that some of his undisciplined attitudes to the game were more than outweighed by his football skills. In the Czechoslovakian senior national team he had to adapt to the players from Sparta Prague, who were the majority, and had to show that he could play good football even without his friends from the Nitra team. The truth is that, even then, he could've played with the biggest stars in the leading European clubs and not be lost among them. It's a pity that he didn't get a better opportunity.

He won the Czechoslovakia Footballer of the Year Award only when there couldn't have been slightest doubt about it. He deserved to win the Slovakia Award too, but never did. To my mind, he is the best and most successful Slovakian footballer of his generation. But he never needed too many opportunities to show how good he was. He was able to take even the smallest chance and to keep his position after that. When he left Nitra to go abroad, I thought, rather naively I must say, that we'd replace him by concentrating more on teamwork. I was wrong. I realised then how good he was. The quality of football produced by the Nitra team went down. He was a complete player and hard to replace. He could play with both feet equally well. He liked to hold on to the ball but at the right moment, with the opposition players closing down on him, he could switch the play with a 50-metre pass. His dribbling was never without purpose, never self-indulgent.

At St. Etienne he was expected to score goals and was played as a striker. As coach of the Czechoslovakia national team I went to St. Etienne to watch him. His coach there, Christian Sarramagne, tried to convince me that it was the right position for him, but I tried to explain to him the role Lubo played in the Nitra team and in the Czechoslovakia national team, and that he wasn't an out-and-out striker but should be left free as a creative player. That was his best role, in which he was most valuable to the team. A tactical straitjacket was never good for him.

As a coach I had some troubles with Lubo, especially when he young, because of his explosive character. He also had trouble with other coaches, and made them work hard for their money. There were times when he could get carried away, playing as if he was possessed, so that any sudden or unfair disruption of the play saw him often respond immediately, without thinking and often improperly. He was impulsive. He had a go at anyone, coaches, team-mates, referee, but in a few seconds he would calm down and everything would be alright.

Even in training games he always played very seriously. When he got the ball he would hold on to it, refusing to pass it to anyone, taking people on, trying new tricks, he was just entertaining himself. Quite often his runs ended with the opposing player fouling him and Lubo would then do the same to the offender. Foul play, even in a training game, is a difficult thing for a coach to handle. The players would be waiting for me, to see what I was going to do, if I was going to deliver justice or reprimand the star player. That depended on how serious the offence was. Mostly, it was enough just to raise my voice a little. Sometimes it was necessary to impose a financial penalty. Once, I even had to send Lubo off; I told him to pack up and go home.

However, deep down Lubo is a very good man and he would be very sorry for his misdemeanours. He was also able to admit that he was wrong. By the next training session we normally had everything sorted out, but more often than not, even as his fame was growing, we had great fun together. We used to analyse the previous match for a long time before training, and I must say that it wasn't too nice to dissect the game sitting in a not exactly pleasant-smelling dressing room. However, after one rather poor match he did go over the top when we were analysing the game. When it was his turn to speak he said, in front everyone, that he didn't need any physical training, all he needed was an occasional game of tennis. Physical training, he said, was for those who can't play and from now on he'd only be doing the ball training.

In this connection I remember another story. Lubo disliked physical training and once he told me: "Coach, why do we have to run so much? Vilo Hyravy told me that in Ostrava all they do is play training games."

The Ostrava coach was Milan Macala and when we started working together with the Czechoslovakian national team, I was waiting for a moment to tell everyone about their poor training sessions in Ostrava. Well, as soon as I did, Macala was up like a shot and headed off to find Hyravy. Hyravy, who was well-known for his practical jokes, told him he was teasing Lubo because he knew that Lubo loved to play training games for hours.

Working with Lubo could also be difficult because we had little or no experience working with players with such an individual personality as he did. During the years of the Communist regime we were taught that no-one was allowed to stand out. The trouble was that Lubo was standing out already then.

To watch Lubo at training was like watching a marvellous show. His ball control was breathtaking, but he didn't just perform at training. There are plenty of players who do that but he was able to do it in difficult games, in front of thousands of spectators. I'd say that in such circumstances he became even more motivated and was able to perform even better.

He was always entertaining spectators. He was famous for his dribbling, going past the players, in his own penalty box, but what he did in the oppostion's half was even better. In a match against Vitkovice, at home, he took control of a high ball with his backside. Everyone on the pitch stopped, amazed at what they had seen and before the Vitkovice defence could recover, Lubo was in front of the goalkeeper but, unfortunately, he shot too wide and missed the target. He deserved a goal for that piece of skill. He was, and still is, every inch a footballer.

I respect him as a person, mainly because he has remained the good-hearted man that he always was. After his misdemeanours at the training sessions, where he put me on the spot as a coach, he'd be back thirty minutes later to apologise: "Coach, you know me. I didn't mean that." And everything was in order.

Before his football skills I'd like to put his personality. He never talked behind someone's back, never gossiped. He always looked for the good side in people. Fame and money never changed him. He remained the same as he was before making it in big-time football. Many supporters were wrong to criticise him for being direct and sincere.

As a coach I always preferred players like Moravcik., always up to something, rather than players who in their career do nothing worth noticing. Moravcik is a footballer–entertainer, like Petras, Adamec, Jokl or Szikora before him, and people remember players like that for decades.

Milan Lesicky, 56, was the coach of Plastika Nitra, taking them to the UEFA Cup. He was the coach of the last Czechoslovakia national team before the country split in 1993. After that he was the coach of the Slovak Under-21 team.

GOING TO FRANCE

A meeting with fellow Czechoslovakian player Peter Kovarcik in the summer of 1989 laid the foundations for Lubo's departure from Nitra the following year, when he joined St. Etienne. Kovarcik visited Lubo at Nitra and the two men spent several hours chatting in the conference room at the stadium.

What Kovarcik had to say would change Lubo's life forever. He told Lubo that a company he was working for was interested and able to find a player like him a big club. This would mean a good income and financial security, not just him but for all his family.

Lubo was stunned as Kovarcik painted a picture of how Lubo's future career might look. He proposed that Lubo should be transferred to Dynamo Kiev where he'd be able to play in the European Cup, and later he'd move to Real Madrid. This was mind-blowing stuff for a player from Mlynarce who had just turned 22, with a few dozen league games and several international caps to his name. Lubo saw it as a challenge, as well as encouragement and inspiration for his future football career.

He went home to tell his father who thought the proposal improbable, the stuff of dreams and beyond belief. Neither of them believed that something like that was possible, but it was 1989, only a few months before Czechoslovakia's Velvet Revolution. This incredible proposal did become a reality of sorts, although Lubo didn't end up in Real Madrid and his career took a different turn.

From that time, Kovarcik and Lubo started working together. They signed a contract and Kovarcik paid Lubo the equivalent of 200,000 crowns in German marks just for signing this contract. Later he invited Lubo to the Forum Hotel in Bratislava where the wife of the then manager of the Telemundi Company had an exhibition of her paintings. This was where Lubo first met Anton Ondrus who, at that time, had his leg in plaster and was contemplating an end to his

football career. Kovarcik hired Ondrus as Lubo's agent; his first task was to find him a new club.
Soon, Ondrus negotiated a pre-contract agreement for Lubo with the French club AS St. Etienne, although it was kept secret at this time. St Etienne's club president André Laurent, came to talk to Lubo before the quarter-final match at the World Cup in Italy, although most of the talking was done by Ondrus because at that time Lubo couldn't speak a word of French.

It could be argued that these circumstances had a negative effect on Lubo's performance in the game. It wasn't that he had lost his motivation thinking about his future but rather the opposite – he became too eager to impress the watching St Etienne president. That eagerness may have, in part, contributed to his rash action which resulted in a red card, but it did not deter St Etienne and they signed Moravcik.

After the World Cup in 1990, Lubo returned to Nitra for a break but he only had 10 days holiday before the French league started. He was convinced that he had made the right decision in joing St Etienne rather than staying at Nitra or

perhaps moving to Sparta Prague. The meeting with Kovarcik had convinced him to move abroad although at the time he didn't know when or how the transfer would become a reality. In 1990, after the Iron Curtain, came down, it all became possible.
Of course, it wasn't that simple. He had to leave his family and it was not easy to say goodbye. It was a tearful farewell. While his wife Zuzana would be joining him in France just a week after his own departure, it was hard to leave his parents and his brother, as well as all his friends.

On Sunday July 8, 1990 there was a farewell party in Mlynarce. Hundreds of Lubo's fans came to see a farewell football game between the Mlynarce first team and the Mlynarce team of golden oldies. The Golden Oldies whipped the senior team 7–2, with Lubo scoring three of their goals.

Soon it was time to go – leaving his homeland, town, family, team-mates and friends to live in another country where he didn't know anyone and couldn't even speak the language. All he knew was that this was the only choice, the only way to continue his football career. Besides, there was no way back now.

Eventually, he got used to his new country and liked the life there, but he wasn't to forget Nitra. His philosophy is that he can live anywhere in the world but home will always be Nitra.

NEW LIFE

Association Sportive de Saint Etienne – Moravcik's new employer were a club with a glorious tradition, having been 10 times winners of the French championship. The incomparable Michel Platini played in the St. Etienne shirt for two years. Now the club hoped for better times ahead.

The first steps in St. Etienne were not easy for Lubo. He couldn't talk to anyone. He couldn't speak English, or French, only a smattering of German. He had neglected languages in high school and at university had done only one short course in German. Besides, German was more or less useless in France, with one exception. His new team-mate John Sivebaek was a Dane and he could speak German and he tried to help the new player in the team settle in. Later, Lubo confessed that he often just pretended to understand what his Danish team-mate tried to tell him. Most of the time he couldn't understand a word.

He thought that St. Etienne itself was wonderful. It was like another world. Everything was strange to him. The Guichard Stadium seemed fantastic as soon as he walked through the gates. He was used to stadia back home with one little stand and nothing else. The Guichard Stadium had four stands all around and capacity for 45,000 spectators. Even as he surveyed the empty stadium he realised that football would be completely different on this stage. It will be great to get used to the place and face the challenge at this stadium, he kept telling himself, full of enthusiasm and resolve. A few days of feeling homesick was replaced by a new-found desire to get on with the job.

Settling down was easier, especially because he could see that the St. Etienne coach Christian Sarramagne wanted him in the team and was instrumental in bringing him to the club. His first experience, however, wasn't the best. St. Etienne went to play a friendly in Geneva, a warm-up game a week before the start of the French season. For Moravcik this was his first game for the team, the first

opportunity to play with his new team-mates. He wanted to do well and make an impression, but during the match he sprained his ankle and had to be taken off. Fortunately, the injury wasn't as serious as it looked.

Lubo felt that right from the start of his time at St Etienne, the club were glad to have him and they did everything they could to make his first months in France as pleasant as possible. The club hired an interpreter for him - a Czech with a vaguely Slovak surname Hron, who emigrated to France from Prague some twenty years ago. He helped Lubo for a whole year, coming to training, travelling with the team on Saturdays and Sundays to wherever the team was playing. He was constantly around, helping and interpreting for him. On the one hand, this was very helpful to Lubo but it also meant that he was making slow progress learning the language himself.

The first six months of the season proved quite difficult. Having had just 10 days rest after the World Cup, Lubo found himself playing in a harder, more demanding league than he was used to in Czechoslovakia, and again the difficulties arose more because of the physical demands than the football ones. It quickly became apparent to Moravcik that he was coping with the new league in terms of mental attitude and technical skills, but physical strength was also a major requirement. It didn't help that the team had started the season poorly, and soon found themselves in the relegation zone. Lubo was fortunate, however, in that the coach retained his faith in the Slovakian player and was convinced that the team's run of bad luck would soon change. Lubo was later able to repay his faith.

Bernard Bosquier, the former French international footballer, was director of football at St Etienne and was instrumental behind the scenes in bringing Moravcik to the club in 1990. Lubo never met him at the time, but 11 years later, Bosquier told him that Lubo was the main reason for his sacking, six months after he signed for the club.

At the time the club president justified the sacking by saying that the team hadn't been doing well and that improvements expected after signing new players hadn't been forthcoming. The president blamed Bosquier for bringing in too many new players - eight including Moravcik; among the others were Cameroon international Pagal who, like Lubo, had played in the quarter-finals of the World Cup in Italy. Bosquier's aim was to strengthen the team by investing in new players and to restore the club to the position it had been at 10 years before - winners of the French league in 1981. His dream was to end the decade of bad results. However, the fact was the club was in a worse position than the previous year. The threat of relegation meant that the director of football had to go, something Lubo only found out about 11 years later. Certainly, Moravcik alone couldn't turn the club's fortunes around but the fact was that St Etienne, with so many new players, just didn't gel.

After 19 league games, Lubo had scored only one goal, a fact that was pointed out to him by the club management. Lubo tried to defend himself: "I did not start winning matches in the first six months in Nitra either," he declared. "I have a contract for four years. No-one can expect miracles from me now. Everything will get better when I settle down."

Then came the winter break. Lubo was able to rest and recharge his batteries before returning to the club's winter training camp. He started to feel that he was getting into good shape. Once the season re-started, St Etienne began to see the real Lubo Moravcik, the player scoring seven goals and making a significant contribution in St Etienne's successful fight against relegation. Lubo played with a great spirit, determined to repay the coach and others at the club who believed in him and helped him in the preceding months. His performances were also praised in the French media. After a match against Paris Saint Germain, one paper published an article about him with the heading Moravcik est magiqu, describing his match performance as masterful.

He could also have no complaints about the St Etienne supporters. They had realised he was a good player and they were ready to accept him from the day he arrived at the club, but when he returned after the winter break and began scoring more goals, his popularity among the fans soared. Lubo also retained his place in the Czechoslovakian national team. In an interview, when asked whether his attitude to the national team has changed, he answered: "Yes, it has. It now means much more to me than before."

In March 1991, he played for Czechoslovakia in a friendly against Poland in Olomouc. The team won 4–0 and Lubo caused a sensation by scoring the second goal with a shot from just outside the centre circle. The following day, under the heading Moravcik learned from Pele, the newspaper Czechoslovak Sport wrote: "When Pele tried to surprise the goalkeeper Victor at the 1970 World Cup in Mexico, Moravcik was still in nursery school. But it seems that he had learned from the great player. Noticing Sidorczuk far out from his goal-line, Moravcik lobbed him with a shot from some 40 metres."

The next season Sarramagne remained as coach at St Etienne. For Lubo this was a much easier season because he had settled down in the team and felt more at home, but still the team's results didn't show a marked improvement. St Etienne were not involved in a relegation battle, but still found themselves stuck in the bottom half of the table.

Sarramagne resigned as coach at the end of the season. Before he left he spoke with Lubo and told him: "You're an outstanding player but you are not effective enough. If you score more goals you'd be even more important for the team." On reflection, Moravcik acknowledges that Sarramagne was right.

After many years in football, Sarramagne thought that this was and still remains Moravcik's greatest shortcoming, a player of such quality should score at least 10–15 goals a season, not 6 or 7 like he actually did.

Part of the reason for this, which Lubo would be the first to admit, was that he never practiced shooting or concentrated on developing his goal-scoring ability. "If I were to start my football career all over again, I'd definitely spend more time in shooting and goal-scoring practice," Moravcik now admits. "The players who score goals are valued most. It doesn't matter how they score, from a penalty or free kicks or from the open play, as long as they do." Lubo was a skilful player, able to use either foot, but never scored many goals. Whenever he assesses his career, Sarramagne's words always come to mind.

Through the eyes of team-mate Jozef Chovanec

I have a good recollection of the first match we played together. It was in November 1987 in Prague. Czechoslovakia were playing Wales in a qualifying game for the 1988 European Championship. I was the captain and Lubo was making his international debut. We won but it wasn't enough to qualify.

It doesn't happen very often that a player in his first international match, and one as important as that, will play so well. Right from the start, Lubo had an impact, he was reliable, able to revitalise the game and confirm his talent. At that time Sparta Prague provided most of the players for the national team. This wasn't because of favouritism, it was just a reality. The national team was always built around a core players from one team, like Dukla Prague, Slovan Bratislava or Spartak Trnava in the past. Moravcik's selection for the national team was no fluke, he showed that he was a top player, his performances convinced everyone. He simply deserved to be in the national team, although he was playing for Nitra, a relatively small club. We all accepted it. He didn't get lost among the majority of players from Sparta. Players accepted him straight away because every team needs a personality like Moravcik.

He confirmed his class in every game we played together. He had incredible vitality, will to win and marvellous ball skills, not to mention a bagful of tricks to bamboozle the opposition players. He had no problem playing one-on-one, taking people on, which is the mark of an outstanding player. He was one of the most skilful players of our generation. He was a crowd puller, people came to watch him play like they did other international stars.

At that time we had a strong national team and confirmed that at the World Cup in Italy. Lubo had a sense for fair-play but sometimes his response to bad decisions could be very impulsive, as the case of his red card in the quarter-finals for kicking his own boot that came off in the tackle by an opposition player proved. Lubo's response was a reflection of his temperament. Many people find it hard to understand that emotions are part of football and usually castigate the players for showing them. Lubo was an emotional footballer.

The fact that, at the age of 36, he's still actively playing for a top club like Celtic is a demonstration of his fantastic attitude. He loves football, it is his life, so he keeps fit. He's a true professional. Later, when I became a coach I could appreciate his qualities, even though I never coached him personally. I think any coach would have him. He'd still walk into the current Czech or other national team. Every player's different, has different qualities but together they make up a team. Moravcik is at the same level with the best players that are currently playing under me in the Czech team.

I watch him and follow his football career, at least from a distance. I'm rather surprised that back home in Slovakia he is still not fully appreciated. Lately he has not even been in the Slovakia squad. I've also heard some criticism of him, which is incomprehensible to me. I think it's unjustified considering his exceptional talent and his attitude to his home country and to the Slovakia national team. He is much more highly regarded abroad as is the case of many others and this does not apply, I think, only to footballers or sportsmen.

We normally do not keep in personal contact but it's always a pleasure when we meet. Recently he came to my and Ivan Hasek's benefit game. Many of our good friends and team-mates turned up and it was a great occasion for me. When I came with the Czech Republic national team to play Scotland in a qualifying game for the 1998 World Cup in France, Lubo helped me a lot, providing invaluable information about Scotland. He came to visit us in our hotel and came to our training sessions. Apart from myself, he still has many friends in the Czech team. What I found is that he is still the same good friend - full of fun, optimism and good spirit.

I am proud to have been, along with Lubo, part of to the same generation of footballers who made up a strong Czechoslovakia national team. I am glad to have met him and played with him in this team and even more so, to have come to know him as a team-mate and as a person.

Jozef Chovanec, 41, former player and captain of the Czechoslovakia national team. He was a key player and, later, a coach of Sparta Prague. At present he is a coach of the Czech Republic national team.

NO TO TAPIE

St Etienne, under new coach Jacques Santini, started the 1992 season is sparkling form and Lubo was a leading light, scoring five goals in the first six games of the season.

It was not surprising, therefore, that he was soon attracting the attention of bigger clubs, and at that time there was no bigger club in France than Olympique Marseille. Through Anton Ondrus he started negotiating with Marseille.

"I didn't have anyone to advise and direct me," says Moravcik. "This should be the role of a FIFA accredited agent. No player these days can do without him. If the agent used to be a footballer he'd be even more important a figure for a player to rely on."

With hindsight, Lubo knows he should have gone to Marseille. It appears to be one of his few football regrets but there are no recriminations. "I still cannot say anything bad about Ondrus or Kovarcik," he admits. Ondrus tried to tie up Moravcik's deal with Marseille but it wasn't easy, and Lubo was torn between ambition and loyalty. He still had a contract with St. Etienne so he felt he couldn't just walk in and tell them: "That's it. I'm leaving."

After two years with the club he had established a good reputation as well as a fantastic rapport with the St Etienne supporters. The club president wouldn't hear about him leaving. His ambition was still to restore the club to its place among France's football elite. In season 1992-93 the team continued to improve and the president announced:"It's make or break for St Etienne."

The fact still remains that Lubo should have left and joined Marseille, but he was unable to make the decision to leave. St Etienne supporters were stopping him in the street, pleading him to reject the offer from Marseille owner Bernard Tapie. Everyone in the club wanted him to stay, no-one told him to leave. Still, Lubo did talk to Tapie on the phone. The Marseille boss congratulated him on his recent performances, including a win in Nantes when Moravcik scored the only goal of the match, and told him: "We'll buy you and you'll become our player."

Lubo said: "I agree, but it doesn't depend on me." He didn't say he wasn't interested in the offer but he was unwilling to push the deal forward himself. If he had insisted that he wanted to go to Marseille, the clubs would have to come to an agreement. He shouldn't have done that, even if it meant upsetting some people at St Etienne. It was his career and his future to think about. At 27 he still had the best years of his playing career ahead of him and a move to Marseille would have benefited him, but eventually, he said no to Tapie and missed out on the chance of a lifetime. Soon after, Olympique Marseille won the European Cup.

Although later, because of the bribery scandal, Marseille were stripped of the European title and relegated to the second division, Lubo thought it wouldn't have significantly affected his career. At worst, the club would sell him, and players from Marseille never went to second-rate clubs. Tapie himself, in their telephone conversation, reminded him that it was closer to Italy from Marseille than from St Etienne. This was a good point - at that time in his football career, Lubo was ready to play at the highest level. That was Serie A.

Still, having decided to stay at St Etienne, 1992 proved to be Moravcik's best year in French football. The respected sports newspaper, France Football, voted him the best foreign player in the first division, and in an interview with the paper, Moravcik said: "To win this title is a great honour, a confirmation of my achievement. I was unknown when I came to St. Etienne, but playing in the French league and getting this award is certainly helping my football career."

Lubo hoped to become an even more important player for St. Etienne and that the club would rise to the top of the league table.

This may be a reason that he didn't pursue the opportunity to join Marseille as strongly as he should have. In another interview for France Football later that year he said: "I do not lack ambitions playing for St. Etienne. It is necessary to have ambitions in the club like that because everyone in St. Etienne remembers the great team of a decade ago. This will push us to do better. I believe this club is capable of winning titles again and play in Europe's Champion's League."

When the interviewer commented that it all depended on him, Moravcik said: "It is not easy for me, especially because it's been like that for some time, but that's football. I'm paid to play. I'm a professional."

He also won recognition back in Czechoslovakia. He won the last federal award for the best footballer of the year in 1992. Jiri Nemec from Sparta Prague, who came second, paid tribute to Moravcik's achievement. "To become an established player in the French league as Lubo did is admirable," said Nemec. "He deserves the title of the best player in Czechoslovakian football."

GOODBYE TO ST. ETIENNE

St. Etienne finished the season in seventh place, just one point away from qualifying for the UEFA Cup. In the French Cup, the club reached the semi-final but in the second leg lost 1–0 to Nantes at home. The players saw themselves going to the final in Paris when Nantes scored the all-important away goal five minutes before the end. The club was so near yet so far from success and this failure, particularly in failing to qualify for Europe, cost the club president André Laurent his job. It was Laurent who tried to convince Lubo that he should stay at St. Etienne and reject Marseille's offer.

Lubo was happy to sign another four-year contract with St. Etienne, but things didn't work out the way he thought. The club was now run by people who didn't appear to rate him as highly as their predecessors had done.

He continued his run of good form until the end of 1993, and praise for his performances was coming from every direction. Sport daily L'Equipe wrote about him after the last game of the season in Monaco: "The man of the match was Moravcik from St Etienne. A classy player with a great anticipation and ability to read the game and, in addition to that, he also scored a goal. Simply a marvellous player."

Lubo appeared settled at the club. He had bought a house just outside St Etienne and looking to the future, he had hopes of finishing his career here. If everything went as planned, at the end of his contract with St. Etienne he'd be 32. By then he'd have spent seven years with the club and could continue his life here, staying with the club in some other capacity, but this plan came to nothing and everything turned out differently. In the second year under Santini, the team's performances were average. At the back of his mind, Lubo kept thinking that by saying no to Marseille he closed the door on the chance to take his career further.

There were still international duties. The last joint team of Czechs and Slovaks failed to qualify for the 1994 World Cup in the USA, while the new Slovakia team was developing slowly, after starting from scratch in 1993. Only he and Peter Dubovsky had previous international experience with Czechoslovakia, but Lubo knew it was necessary to keep on fighting, without any thoughts of giving up. It seemed to him that his chances to further his career at top-level European football were much slimmer after rejecting a move to a big club like Marseille.

Things at St Etienne did not help during this period of retrospection. While his own performances remained impressive, good results can only be attained with a strong team and after Santini left St Etienne, a number of established players left too. They were replaced by players from lower divisions, and under these conditions Lubo's prospects for further development as a footballer didn't look that good.

At times he was becoming nostalgic, thinking about the good times in his beloved Nitra, remembering the easier, less pressurised football that was played there. He recognised that on a professional level, the football in France was of a higher standard, especially considering the set-up and organisation of clubs, the speed and tempo on the football pitch, publicity in the media and the big money involved. He also realised that, lately, he hadn't played for the sheer joy of it.

"In France I was always closely marked by the opposition teams," he explained. "Sometimes I felt the opposition defenders would follow me to the dressing room. The games were becoming really hard work. Our play became sweaty, more orientated towards strength, there was plenty of one-on-one tackling. I felt much better playing against top teams who played with creative rather than destructive tactics. Back home, playing at the Zobor ground with Nitra, it was great. With Zolo Molnar and Robo Jez in midfield, we were hitting it about, passing the ball, enjoying our football. We scored plenty of goals, opposition sides didn't know whom to mark. It's a pity I didn't have players like that with me in St. Etienne."

At the end of the 1995 season, St. Etienne were only saved from relegation because Marseille were demoted to the lower division. Next season, though, nothing could save them and the club was relegated. At the start of the season, things hadn't looked so bad. In preparation for the season, St. Etienne even beat AC Milan 2–1 and Lubo scored both goals. The team was excellent that day, and he was one of the best players on the pitch which, by that time, was not unusual. The trouble was that the team's performance in pre-season games wasn't continued in the league. The squad also became depleted and the club went through financial difficulties with debts close to 15 million francs.

Moravcik was clearly the team's best player. After the first half of season he came second to Djorkaeff in a poll for the best player in the French league by France Football. He was also selected in the best team of the season, but he couldn't save St Etienne on his own. The end of the season was the culmination of a long-term crisis in the club. When it became clear that St. Etienne were going to be relegated, Moravcik heard from Marseille again. By that time Bernard Tapie had left and the club was on way back to the first division. He met with the management in Marseille and after talks his transfer to Marseille was 90% agreed. It only required the approval of the Marseille team manager to secure the deal.

The day he was due to go on holiday with his family to Tunisia, Moravcik suddenly heard from his agent, an older and experienced Frenchman. He had asked the agent to get him out of the contract with St Etienne because he didn't want to play in the second division, and the contract still had another year to run. The agent promised to do his best to ensure Moravcik could stay in the first division with Olympique Marseille. Now he turned up at Moravcik's door. He was not alone, he brought Bastia officials with him. The officials told him that, according to newspapers, Marseille were not interested in Moravcik because the manager, Gérard Gili, had different plans, and, there and then, they offered him contract with Bastia. He knew Bastia, having played there several times. The club, based on the island of Corsica, had a small but nice football ground. It was always a difficult place to play an away game.

He hesitated before definitely saying 'yes'. He couldn't agree a financial deal with Bastia officials as they were unable to match the money he was getting in St Etienne. After a long debate he thought: Why not? I'll sign for them for a year, then we'll see. He was 31, it was important to keep playing in the first division, with a reasonable team, and, most importantly, with a club whose coaches and officials wanted him. After a year he would find a better and longer contract somewhere else which would be more beneficial, in football and financial terms. In the end he packed up, sold the house and moved the family to Bastia.

He went to Bastia determined to work hard and do as best as he could for his new team. He realised that money was not that relevant in this situation. It was more important to play for a club where he could enjoy his football. He told himself: "In a year I'll be a free agent. Then I'll decide what to do next."

Through the eyes of his wife Zuzana Moravcikova

"If I should describe him in a few words I'd just say that Lubo is a good man."

At first my relationship with Lubo started very slowly. We went together to technical school, and were in the same year. Although we knew one another since we were children, we were just classmates, there was nothing between us. We just liked one another as friends.

In the last year at school, just before the final exam, we went on a school trip to Prague where we spent a lot of time together. We wandered through the town, went to see historical monuments and I was pleasantly surprised seeing Lubo's interest. This was probably the beginning of our relationship, which became closer at the party after the final exam. Lubo walked me home and after that we started going out together regularly.

I've always liked sport. I grew up in a sporting family. My father was in a boxing club, I used to play handball, and my brother is now a top football referee in Slovakia. It impressed me to see how seriously Lubo took his football. This was at the beginning of his football career before he became famous. I wasn't to know how far he would go in football, the fact that he chose football as his career wasn't that important to me and it wasn't affecting our relationship. At first I wasn't interested in football that much. Only, through Lubo have I come to like this fascinating game and become a fan.

From the beginning I liked Lubo's character and personality. He was happy, friendly, pleasant and sincere but I could see that he was ambitious too. What he thought was important to him he would go for, and wouldn't let anyone dissuade him, but I still keep telling him that his environment, with all his friends and relatives, helped to make him the person he is and helped him to achieve what he did. When we started going together he didn't yet play for a first division team, not mention the national team or a big club abroad. He achieved all this with me beside him so I like to think that I made at least a small contribution to it. He values this and recognises it, which gives me a good feeling.

Lubo has always discussed everything with me although I must say that if he gets something into his head, he'll do everything to convince me that his solution is the best; and most of the time it is. I went with him wherever he decided to pursue his football career. He was always among the people, always busy. It is easier for him to learn a new language and to get used to a new environment. I've always respected his ambitions, although the frequent moving and getting used to new places is not always easy, especially with little children.

When we left Slovakia our son Matus was just two-years old, while our daughter Roberta was born in France. Everything became more difficult when the children started school. We were on the move, living in different countries - France, Germany, Scotland.

Once I did stand my ground, though. This was when he decided to leave Germany because he had an offer to join Celtic. The kids had started school in Germany, in the middle of the school year, so I told him: "All right, you go to Glasgow and I'll join you with the children later, once we see that it is a more permanent solution, not just for a few weeks." I actually returned to Slovakia and put the children into a Slovakian school. We didn't move to Glasgow until six months later.

I often keep thinking, especially when he comes home tired and disappointed, that he could finish playing football and start spending spend more time with family, but so far I haven't voiced this opinion aloud. Lubo is now more composed and calmer than at the beginning of his football career. This comes with age, I think. In his younger days he couldn't stand losing, he'd be cross, throwing his

boots about, then come home disappointed and in a bad mood. I'd leave him to calm down and we wouldn't talk about football for a while.

He is very popular now. He has fans, including female admirers waiting for him after the game. It could make me jealous but I've never had any reason to be. I like it that people are interested in him. I don't mind them asking for his autograph or having a picture taken with him. I trust Lubo. I think he is a family man and really cares for those close to him.

He is meticulous, almost pedantic and orderly. In this respect he is not a typical man. He loves the children but sometimes he doesn't have time to be with them. Basically, he is quite lenient with them, while I am the strict one in the family. I don't want them just to get everything they ask for, I want them to be appreciate what they have.

So far we have had to adapt ourselves to Lubo's career, which is understandable, but I hope that his priority will be his family, particularly the children, when he stops playing football. I'm looking forward to spending more time with him. I want us to return to France so the children can finish their schooling there. Here, in Scotland, they go to the local school but they have a French teacher and still keep up their French studies. They record their assignments on cassettes and send them to France for marking.

In many respects life with a professional football is not different from any other - sometimes it's pleasant, sometimes it's not. There's a lot of happiness but sometimes we have to deal with problems and difficulties that are specific to our life but do not exist in other families. I respect Lubo for what he achieved. It's a beautiful feeling to sit in a packed stadium, with the spectators shouting his name. I'm proud of him, but most of all I like him the way he is. If I should describe him in a few words I'd just say that Lubo is a good man.

Zuzana Moravcikova, 36, graduated from technical school, now stays at home bringing up her two children, son Matus and daughter Roberta. She married Lubo in 1987.

LEG IN PLASTER

News of Moravcik's signing caused great excitement in Bastia. Everyone was looking forward to the arrival of a footballer of his calibre, and the welcome he received when he arrived on the island of Corsica was just fantastic; coaches, team-mates and supporters immediately made him feel part of the club. He was free to use Bastia's facilities to rest and recharge his batteries before the coming season. He started pre-season training and was working very hard and with enthusiasm, realising this was probably his last chance to sell himself to a top-level European club.

The team started well, playing marvellous football. By sheer coincidence, the first home game was against Marseille, which Bastia won 2–0, with Moravcik scoring the first goal. Everything seemed to suggest that this was going to be his best season ever. At 31 he was in top shape, physically and mentally, but just when everything was going so well disaster struck.

Up until this point in his career, he had managed to stay relatively free of injuries, but in the game against Monaco on October 12, 1996 he injured his knee in a clash with Emmanuel Petit. It was a serious setback and put Moravcik out of football for more than three months – 133 days to be precise. However, because of the inflammation of cartilage it took longer for him to start playing again. After ten days of intensive training, without any warm-up game, the coach Fréderic Antonetti, already missing several players through injury, put him in the team to face Nancy in a league game. He took to the field with a steel plate and six screws in his knee.

The Bastia supporters were delighted to see him back and he received a warm welcome, but there were nagging doubts in Moravcik's mind; he felt that his injury still wasn't completely healed. During the match he didn't avoid any tackle and didn't feel too uncomfortable, but he did feel a pain afterwards, though he just put it down to tiredness after the match. These feelings persisted throughout the following weeks.

His return to playing was tougher than he had expected. He had to push himself to get through the training, and he didn't stop worrying when he took to the field before a game. After the warm-up it was fine but any short breaks made it worse. Half-time was becoming a nightmare and meant that the first 10 minutes of the second-half was sheer torture.

Somehow Lubo managed to keep playing until the end of the season. At the time of his return, Bastia were in an excellent position, lying third in the league table. The UEFA Cup was a distinct possibility and they still had an outside chance to qualify for the Champions League. In the end, they missed out on the Champions League and were also denied the chance to play in the UEFA Cup by a single point.

So Lubo was now a free agent. He had several offers, including another one from Bastia, who wanted him to stay, but he decided to go to FC Sion in Switzerland. The Swiss club were due to play in the qualifying round for a place in the Champions League and he still harboured hopes of playing in this prestigious competition. Besides, Sion was in the French-speaking part of Switzerland, which meant that the children could go to a French school, but there was still one more game to play before he could consider the season closed.

In June, Slovakia played Yugoslavia in a World Cup qualifier. There were only five minutes left in the game when the Yugoslav player Mijatovic caught Lubo's knee in a sliding tackle – exactly on the sore spot. In the following month Lubo's knee remained painful but he wasn't sure to what extent this was the result of the tackle against Mijatovic. Little did he know just how serious his situation was.

When Lubo reported for pre-season training with Sion, he knew his injury had still not cleared completely; the strong pain in his knee was now a constant companion. The team was training twice a day in preparation for the coming season. He went through the physical training in the morning, doing all the exercises, including jumps. Then he went home, had a rest, and went back to stadium for ball practice in the afternoon. The coach divided the squad into two teams and they played a training game. His knee was still sore but he disregarded the pain, accepting it as the part of his present condition; he got used to living with it.

The training game would always end with a 'Golden Goal' finish and Moravcik hit a shot with his injured leg. It was sore but, then again, it was what he had become used to. Next day he went for a medical examination, which was just a routine check-up of the players. The result, however, was shocking. After an X-ray, the doctor told him that his leg was broken, in the same place as before. It was only the steel plate and the screws which held it in place - Moravcik had gone through two weeks training suffering from a broken leg.

"I have a suspicion that the fracture wasn't properly healed in the first place," Moravcik admitted. "That's why it remained painful. Now I have to come to a conclusion that it's possible to keep training with a broken leg, provided that it's held with screws. There's no need to have six screws, even five would do, as was my case. One screw was actually broken!"

It was a terrible situation, both for Moravcik and Sion. The player was out for four months and so was the dream of the Champions League. It also left Moravcik in limbo. While he had signed a contract with Sion, the president of the club no longer wanted to keep the injured player, and so never paid Bastia the transfer fee that had been set by a UEFA committee. In this situation, Bastia were left with no choice but to cancel the contract with Sion and take Moravcik back.

Lubo had to face another operation, which was more difficult this time because he had to have a bone graft to replace about 2 centimetres of the fractured bone. This also meant a period of convalescence of five months. Thankfully, the operation was successful and he was able to extend his summer holidays back home in Slovakia. He returned to Bastia in September for the beginning of the school year. The target he set himself was to get himself back into shape by the winter break and start playing again in the second half of the season. The plan for ending his football career was getting somewhat complicated.

ON STRIKE IN BASTIA

Bastia gave him another chance. He hoped to repay the club by playing at least in the second half of the season and help them to get into one of the European competitions that the club so narrowly missed out on the previous year. He continued training hard and in December, just before Christmas, he appeared again in a league game.

Many people were advising Moravcik not to rush his comeback, especially considering the bad experience he had before with his injury, and concentrate instead on getting back to full training after the New Year, but Lubo felt good and, most all, he missed football. His knee was fine, he felt no pain.

However, his comeback didn't turn out as he hoped. The team had been playing well up until then and had qualified for the UEFA Cup via the Intertoto Cup in the summer. After Lubo returned to the team, they lost three games in a row. He was unhappy and blamed himself for the defeats; it didn't matter that it was a team game, Moravcik always tended to blame himself if the things didn't go well.

To make matters worse, he had a disagreement with Antonetti, even though he had a great deal of respect for him. He still regards Antonetti as the best coach he played under in France. They had an argument and, without really meaning it, the coach told him: "If you don't like, you can go." Lubo's response to the ultimatum was to stop coming to training. He stayed at home for a week, thinking over the situation. It wasn't easy to make a comeback after two fractures and he wasn't getting any younger either. He considered his future, and thought about returning home to Slovakia. He was effectively on strike in Bastia, though publicly, the club explained that his absence was due to persistent injury.

He was in contact with Spartak Trnava. The coach there was Dusan Galis and the manager was a man from Nitra, Stefan Batalik. Lubo was seriously thinking about playing the rest of the season with Trnava and then going to Austria for the remainder of his football career.

The week's rest has helped him, however. He had just needed more time to decide what he really wanted to do. "What really got me was that after four months training like mad trying to get myself into shape, I couldn't do a thing right when I started playing," he explained. "It made me nervous and really put me off. So I took a week off without the coach's or the club's consent, but there was never a question of me not going back and sorting the things out with the club."

After a week he made a dramatic return to the stadium, arriving at the ground on roller skates, riding along the skating path that leads around the Bastia stadium, right in the middle of a training session. The players and the coach, too, were bemused.

"We'll talk about everything later," was all that Antonetti said. At a meeting later, they sorted out their differences. Lubo insisted that after twice breaking his leg it would be necessary for him to change his style of play and, also, that his role in the team had to be re-defined. He felt that his previous role required more running rather than playing football. The two men were in agreement. For the next match the coach changed the tactics, with Lubo is a new role, and the changes reaped an instant reward. Bastia beat Monaco 1–0 and Moravcik felt relieved; a weight was off his shoulders and he was determined to do his best for Bastia for the remainder of the season.

There still remained the question of where to go after Bastia. While Lubo felt some sort of moral obligation to the club because of the way they had stood by him during his injury problems, they still wouldn't offer him anything more than a one-year contract while he wanted something longer. He was now 33 and still felt he had a lot to offer. A new challenge was just round the corner.

Through the eyes of team-mate Jan Kocian

"Playing with Lubo, I could close my eyes and pass the ball to either of his feet. He could also shoot with his left or right foot. Neither was used just for standing on."

The first time Lubo really drew my attention as a player was in the Slovakia Cup final in Trnava, when Nitra played Dunajska Streda. He took a penalty and missed it. I noticed he took the penalty with his left foot, which was strange since I had always thought of him as being right-footed. Anyway, he kicked it with his left foot and I thought: "Stupid bugger, to miss a chance like that, what a risk to take." I thought it was careless and irresponsible of him.

What I didn't know then was that Lubo really was one of those genuine two-footed players and I was able to see this for myself afterwards on many occasions. I haven't come across many footballers as talented as he is. In Germany, it was Brehme who was thought to be truly two-footed but his right foot was just a touch better than his left. In a team players are normally aware who is stronger on which foot, and they pass the ball to them on that side. They know that some players prefer to get the ball to, say, their right foot in order to take a shot. With Lubo it didn't matter. I could close my eyes and pass the ball to either of his feet. He could also shoot with his left or right foot. Neither was used just for standing on."

When I was being critical of his failure to convert the penalty in Trnava, I didn't know that our football careers would run together at certain points. A short time later, my team, Banska Bystrica, was playing in Nitra and from there I travelled with Lubo to join the Czechoslovakia Olympic team.

There were not many Slovaks in any of the national teams at that time so we stuck together and became an inseparable pair. We used to share a room on our trips with the Olympic team. Later, with Vlado Weiss and Peter Fieber, there were four Slovak players in what was then a very strong Olympic team, coached by Milos Kvacek and Jozef Jankech. The four of us became friends, and remain so to this day.

Unfortunately, we didn't make it to the Olympic Games in Seoul, having lost the deciding qualifier against Yugoslavia. After that our football careers went different ways for a while. I managed to get transferred to St. Pauli in Germany in 1988, while Lubo, who was still a young player, stayed at Nitra. I thought that my days with Czechoslovakia national team were over but quite soon things took a different turn. I met up again with Lubo in the national team under coach Jozef Venglos. We got to play together in many important international matches and we made it to the World Cup in Italy. Lubo was by then one of the best players in Czechoslovakia and a key member of the national team.

Lubo always lived for football, his enthusiasm was just unbelievable. He was an elegant ball player, with no brute force but lightness in his game. He didn't like to lose, he couldn't bear it and on such occasions he could be critical of others but mostly of himself. He was always open and straightforward, and could tell others what he thought.

He rejected German football where I settled and where I still work as a coach. Whenever I think of Lubo I always remember his unsuccessful spell in Germany. I'm sure it's not a question of whether he was suited to the German style of football or not, he simply couldn't get on with the style of the Duisburg team nor with the tactics used by the coach Funkel.

This was later confirmed by Sepp Eichkorn, who was then Funkel's assistant and also my coach at one stage. When I spoke to him recently, Eichkorn admitted that it was incomprehensible to him why Moravcik was asked to fulfil various tactical roles rather than be allowed to display his undoubted qualities for the benefit of the team.

Eichkorn, who is now coach with Magath in Stuttgart, also told me that Lubo was the best footballer he ever saw. The fact is that Duisburg's style just wasn't suitable for a player like Moravcik. It was based on physical strength and never-say-die attitude, the attributes of all the teams that Funkel coached. Lubo just didn't fit into his concept.

When Lubo was with Duisburg, I was back playing in Slovakia. We often talked on the phone and I hoped everything would turn out well for him. I couldn't understand what the problem was. Players like Moravcik are rare and therefore welcome in Germany. It is a well-know fact that German clubs normally look for creative players abroad, and Lubo is a creative player who can run and control the game. Even now I'm still convinced that a player of his qualities should have found place in a German team without any problems.

Then again, I think it was a great piece of luck that he got an opportunity to play for a big club like Celtic, where his skills found their use and he was able to show what a great footballer he is. I just admire him, especially for the way he took his chance after his unpleasant experience in Germany.

We kept in contact at that time so I know he was determined to leave Germany. He had some offers from Slovakian clubs and did consider returning home. I told him not to because, as I found out from my own experience, in Slovakia jealousy and hatred are not far apart and Lubo's experience was, I think, similar. He is quick-tempered and impulsive, like myself, and I thought he wouldn't stay longer than two weeks. I kept telling him that while he still had an opportunity to play abroad, he should take it, and that at his age he could still play football at the highest level. What also helped was that for a long time he was able to stay free of serious injuries; his other advantage is that he knows how to prepare himself for every match.

I've always said that Lubo should have been voted Slovakia's player of the year at least seven times in a row, and I still believe that. I have seen him playing in France quite a few times, and I also know, from my own experience, how frequently and how hard the players have to work. The way in which he established himself as a top player and the length of time he kept himself at this level seem incredible to me. It's time for him to get greater recognition in Slovakia.

Not many people know him well, either as a player or as a person. The reason for his qualities and attitudes not being recognised as they should is, in my view, that there's not enough information about him. He was always happy to return, looking forward to pulling on the shirt of the national team. He'd often told me: "They can call me at midnight or whenever and I'll be on my way." He's an emotional person and finds it hard to accept any injustice. Abroad he just got used to expressing his opinion but back home this is seen as arrogance on his part. So while he's not exactly unwelcome, he's thought to be difficult to deal with, which is a great pity.

When he started talking about ending his football career, he often suggested to me, half seriously, half in jest, that we both should go back to Slovakia, get hold of a club there and put together a good team. He would like to be the club's president and I should be the coach. I doubt this will ever happen, but then again, you never know. All I know is that I'd like to be a coach in a club where he was president.

Jan Kocian, 41, a former Czechoslovakia player, was later a coach of several first division teams in Slovakia. He is now an assistant coach in FC Cologne in Germany.

A FLOP IN DUISBURG

An offer from the German Bundesliga was unexpected. The coach of MSV Duisburg, Friedheim Funkel, came to watch him play and after the match they had a long meeting, discussing the prospect of Moravcik moving to Germany; a two-year contract was arranged by FIFA agent Peter Telek. Moravcik decided to go to Germany.

The move appealed to him. Duisburg was a small, modest club, an ideal platform for Moravcik to demonstrate his undoubted qualities as a player. Besides, not many 33-year olds got the offer to play in the Bundesliga. He saw it as a challenge and wanted to show that he was still good enough to play in one the biggest football leagues in Europe. He was ready to make one more debut before ending his football career. He was always looking for motivation, not just a contract and money.

He and Zuzana found a private French school in Dusseldorf - about 20 km from Duisburg - so the children could continue their schooling in French but also learn German, and when the family moved into their new house, everything appeared to be going well. However, Lubo soon began to have doubts. He went through pre-season training without any problems even though the work was hard. One week they did nothing else except physical training and running. He could handle that, of course, whenever necessary, but increasingly he had the feeling that the team didn't trust him, that his team-mates were somehow not convinced of his ability. He sensed that he was getting in their way.

Yet he thought that he was brought to strengthen the team, as he did when he came to Bastia two years earlier. The coach at Bastia had announced in front of the other players that Moravcik wasn't brought to do all the work for the team but to provide extra qualities. Moravcik chose Duisburg for the same reason. The previous year they had enjoyed a relatively good season, with no threat of relegation, and getting to the final of the German Cup guaranteed them a place in Europe. Lubo, therefore, believed he was joining a solid team that he would give something extra to. Sadly, this was never the case. His team-mates were openly distrustful of him. The coach told Moravcik he had absolute belief in him and saw him as the club's number one player but never in front of the other players. He was just another player.

"I need the coach to believe in me and to rely on me but he must help me as well," explained Moravcik. "I had some misgivings after the difficult pre-season training, I didn't feel well and I was tired. I decided to grit my teeth and bear it. I thought, I'll wait and see what happens after the first few matches."

His doubts increased after the first match, a warm-up game against Turkish side Trabzonspor. In front of a large crowd, Moravcik was left on the bench until the second-half. Then, at last, the Bundesliga started, with Duisburg at home to Eintracht Frankfurt on the opening day of the season. Moravcik played from the start, on the left of midfield in a free role and he had an impressive game. Moravcik was chosen in the team of the week, and German newspapers wrote positively about his performance. The Kickers magazine even voted him man-of-the-match, declaring: "Moravcik was just magical. The hard-working Slovakian player, with marvellous skills, was also very inventive. The 33-year-old initiated several moves which brought applause from the crowd. He was strong in one-on-one clashes and his passing was excellent."

The SID agency was similarly appreciative: "Moravcik had a great game. He laid some marvellous balls to his forwards and effectively controlled the game. Quite rightly, he was applauded by the crowd. He is a great addition to the team. In the Bundesliga there are not many creative players able to control the game like Moravcik."

The Duisburg coach also spoke well of Moravcik's performance, but his statements were more guarded, unlike the club manager Gerd Merheim who declared: "There's no doubt that Lubo is a world class player."

Moravcik felt relieved. He was satisfied with his performance and felt confident that the coach would now appreciate what the 20,000 crowd had. He was wrong. This was probably the only match he would like to remember from his short spell in Germany. From then on, he never seemed to play in the same position two games in a row; one match he was up front, the next he was in midfield. In one game he was substituted at half-time for not following his man, this despite the fact that Duisburg were leading 1–0.

"I was told to mark a player and follow him whenever he got the ball and headed towards our goal. No-one else but me had to mark that player. I couldn't understand the system," he complained after the match.

From the first moment he arrived at the airport he felt that the people were very cold, in general and towards him, compared with St Etienne where the president had waited for him with a limousine, or Bastia, where people were simply delighted he was there. In Duisburg the attitude was - you are a professional player, we pay you, so you'll do what you are told. Lubo wasn't used to this attitude. He never liked this sort of approach and was unable to hide it.

After his substitution for failing to mark one of the opposition players, Lubo realised there was no point wasting his time in Duisburg. He couldn't enjoy this sort of football. I'll go somewhere else or pack it in, he thought, weighing up the two alternatives. Then he went and told the Duisburg officials that he wanted to leave. He gave them a week for an answer.

There was a possible offer of a move to Japan, to join up with a former Bastia coach but so far it wasn't definite. Duisburg hadn't paid a transfer fee to Bastia as Moravcik had been out of contract. Instead they had paid him a signing on fee, which he promised to pay back; he did, later. It wasn't easy for his family because they were on the move again, but with Lubo not enjoying his football, moving on seemed the best thing to do.

He continued training that week, and on the Friday asked the club if they had made a decision; he wanted to go to Japan. The club's answer was a definite no. Lubo was equally forthright with his answer. "Very well, thank you, I'm retiring." He said, and he left.

Next day the team travelled to their pre-match camp to prepare for a league game. Moravcik stayed at home. The official club announcement was that he was injured but, of course, there was nothing wrong with him. On the Monday he left to join up with the Slovakia team in Bratislava. Duisburg threatened to stop him playing for Slovakia. At first he was afraid they would carry out their threat but in the end they backed down.

"At any rate, after that I was described in the German newspapers as some sort of maverick," said Moravcik. "When I came back to Duisburg, there were TV cameras at the airport, the media tried to ridicule my position, but I decided to leave them to it."

It convinced him even more that he was doing the right thing. On the international scene, the credibility of German football was declining at this time. He thought the Germans should do something to improve the type of football that was now being played in the country. He had always felt he should try to provide attractive football and he refused to adjust to German football. He always made his own decisions, although he would never claim they were always the correct ones. This time, though, he felt he had made the right decision.

LUBO SIGNS FOR CELTIC

Who is the best player you have ever played against?

"I didn't have the chance to play against Maradona, Ronaldo or Rivaldo so it is difficult to pinpoint somebody. I did play against Zidane but he was much younger then and not the great name he is now. In Scotland my most difficult opponent was Jorg Albertz of Rangers."

The official records state that Lubomir Moravcik signed for Celtic on October 27, 1998 but the deep-seated background to a then unknown Slovakian internationalist arriving in the East End of Glasgow was far reaching and the roots of the story stretched back some 17 months.

Causality, providence, call it what you will but due to the very fickle nature of football, destiny plays a decisive role in the sport and while fortune smiled on Celtic in the eventual capture of Lubo's signature, fate cast its grim shadow on others who inadvertently paved the road to Paradise for one of the best midfielders ever to wear the green and white.

That 17-month phase began with the appointment of Jock Brown as Football General Manager in June 1997 but the seeds of scorn that greeted almost every major arrival at Celtic Park in the intervening period were planted years, if not decades, before. The arrival of Graeme Souness at Ibrox slap bang in the middle of the 1980s powered the wheels of a revolution in Scottish football, a dialectic cycle that was spinning away from Celtic faster than the powers that be at Parkhead could comprehend - or would even admit.

Despite Rangers' spending power, they were buying big and bucking the trend by buying from outside Scotland, Celtic rallied and lifted the League and Scottish Cup Double in the glorious Centenary Year of 1987/88. Complacency set in at board level though and the men who pulled the strings failed to support manager Billy McNeill's plea to spend money and strengthen the squad to any degree of comparison with the reform at Ibrox.

The writing was on the wall and it wasn't going to make for good reading for the Celtic faithful. The following season the Scottish Cup was won again but the Celtic legions were possibly more gleeful at halting Rangers' bid for the Treble than actually lifting the trophy itself. Such was the state of Old Firm play at the time and Celtic were ripe for the taking by press and opposition alike. The football press are not known for ignoring someone when they are down – they would rather give them a good kicking and Celtic must have been wearing 'Kick Me Here' signs on the backs of their shorts.

Every dog has its day and while Rangers were wearing the blue ribbons at Crufft's, Celtic were making more headlines than Rottweiler Devil Dogs and much of the blame lay not in the offices of the tabloids but from within the hallowed portals of Celtic Park itself. Celtic were digging their own grave and the media donned the black of professional mourners with a taste for the juicy morsels available at the feeding frenzy after every all-too common wake.

The 'Celtic in Crisis' headlines may not have made cheery reading for the fans but they did play a crucial part in a sea change at the club both on and off the field. McNeill left the managerial hot-seat followed by Liam Brady, and Lou Macari while fan power overturned the old board and Fergus McCann took over the reins at boardroom level. Tommy Burns came in as manager, McCann raised the historic share issue and a magnificent stadium rose from the ashes of a once proud reputation that had gone up in smoke. However, the only on-field tangible success was another Scottish Cup win in 1995 as Rangers ran away with title after title, the natives were restless and the scribes still sharpened their pens on the woes of Celtic. Burns paid the price and departed the turmoil as a club who had employed only four managers in its first 90 years of existence was now becoming very adept at producing job descriptions at the drop of a hat.

It was then that McCann pulled something else out of the hat by procuring the services of Jock Brown as the club's first ever Football General Manager and even before the lawyer and former football commentator had time to get his feet under the table, the press had a field day with the appointment. To be fair to the press, in the previous years they had always given Celtic time to be failures, now they were going for the jugular while Rangers were still in the ascendancy and any appointment, on or off the field, was therefore open to the widest immediate scrutiny.

Coming from a journalistic environment, Brown was openly viewed as poacher turned gamekeeper and the fact that his selection wasn't overly approved by many Celtic fans merely added fuel to a fire that was already aflame with passion. He also played his job remit to the letter and leaks to the press all but dried up as Celtic pulled down the shutters in their search for Burns' replacement.

Every possible name for the Celtic Park post had been bandied about in the press but when Dutchman Wim Jansen walked in to the boardroom to face the media for the first time as Celtic manager there was general bewilderment. Among the pick of the headlines was 'The second worst thing to hit Hiroshima', a reference to Jansen's previous post in Japan, a taunt which rivalled the 'Joke Brown' heading when the new General Manager arrived little more than 10 days earlier.

Jansen proved to be a big hit with players and fans though and securing the Championship to halt Rangers beating Celtic's proud record of nine titles in a row as well as lifting the League Cup afforded him hero status and likewise the press duly accepted the new manager. All was not well in the inner sanctum though and the antipathy between Brown and Jansen was hardly the best-kept secret in town. Rather than cross the road to avoid each other they were more likely to cross the road to hit each other and just two days after lifting the title, the Dutchman quit the post.

The fact that Brown remained while Jansen departed did not go down well with the Celtic devotees and the press quite naturally twisted the knife further. Once more the fans spent the close season scouring the papers to glean news on any possible candidates and there were plenty to choose from. Egil Olsen, Gerard Houllier and a certain Martin O'Neill were among the many connected with the post but yet again the guesses proved to be wide of the mark and yet again there was an air of incomprehension as the new man was paraded on July 17, 1998.

Dr Jozef Venglos was and is highly respected among coaching circles throughout the entire world but he wasn't a household name in Scotland and his unfortunate learned title presented the press with another field day. As expected, 'Dr Who?' screamed the next day's headlines and once again a naïve outsider was introduced to the parasitic world of football reporting Old Firm-style where, if your team is not the flavour of the month then you are tarred with the same brush even if you are just off the taxi from Glasgow Airport.

There was a feeling that Celtic could have signed Rivaldo, Zidane and brought in Superman as player/manager but as long as Brown had something to do with the appointments there would be questions raised.

How much ice this cut with Dr Jo is debatable but no matter how much he realised the press were gunning for Brown rather than him it couldn't have made his task any easier although he did present an almost too civil air of tact and diplomacy that was clearly missing previously when the sparks were flying between Brown and Wim Jansen.

On the whole, new players were not subject to the same level of scrutiny but as Rangers ploughed on spending xyz millions on this player and that, generally household names to boot, the onus was on Celtic to dig deep in the pocket and furnish Dr Jo with some cash for a big name player to level the scales slightly.

This then was the world to which another innocent newcomer was presented when Dr Jo signed his fellow Slovak Lubomir Morvacik to the ranks three months later and it was clear from the initial press reaction that Lubo didn't fit the bill on a number of issues. Despite 74 caps for Czechoslovakia and Slovakia his name hardly rolled off the tongue when your average Scottish punter discussed the merits of European football, Celtic shelled out only £300,000 for an unknown quantity when rivals Rangers were forking out millions and the straw that broke the camel's back was that the new guy was 33-years-old.

It would appear that Celtic and had signed an anonymous geriatric who would be lucky to last a game never mind the rest of the season but Dr Jo knew something the rest of us didn't, the ball was in his court and as we were soon to find out, with Lubo on the job it would be difficult for them to get the ball back.

He arrived as an innocent abroad from a short time with Germany's MSV Duisburg after spells in France with St Etienne and Bastia but even if he didn't know why, he was certainly aware that his arrival at Celtic was selling newspapers.

"I didn't take it personally at all, " recalled Lubo, "I didn't speak English and I didn't read the newspapers so I was a little bit ignorant of what was being said but I was concentrating on my football and obviously I was really focusing on playing well. I felt a big responsibility to Dr Venglos to pay him back for the faith he had in me. He gave me the opportunity and I didn't want to disappoint him.

"I don't really feel that the papers went over the top and the flak didn't give me something to prove as I didn't feel any animosity towards the press because as I said I didn't speak English so couldn't read the newspapers. I was too absorbed in my goal to come to Celtic and try to do my best"

Aside from playing an obviously vital role in signing Lubo, Dr Jo was a national hero in Slovakia and a major influence on the career of a young and developing Moravcik. "I have great respect for Dr Venglos," said Lubo, " because he was really the first coach in my life who showed me the correct road ahead I had to take in football if I wanted to gain success. Especially in my international career which was very successful for me with him, and the World Cup in 1990 was really a big moment in my career and for that he was very important.

"He was vital at both ends of my career, in the beginning and at the end as he brought me here to Celtic. He is very much a legend back home and at the end of the millennium there was a poll and he was voted Slovakian Trainer of the Century. The trophy was presented to Dr Venglos by Jozef Masopust who was voted in as Czech Player of the Century. So he was voted in as the best coach ever in the history of Slovakian football and he is quite simply the biggest coach in our game."

The move to Celtic and Dr Jo presented Lubo with the opportunity of at least a bit of stability after a non-too productive liaison in Duisburg with five games played in just under three months for MSV and that was something he was keen to avoid in Glasgow.

"There wasn't a good under-standing relationship with the coach," he said, "when I went there I understood I was to be an important part of the team. He promised me something and I didn't feel he fulfilled his

promise. I wasn't happy with that and at my age, 33 at the time, I decided I didn't want to play football if I wasn't happy. I had to leave the club."

Duisburg were inconceivably utilising the player in a defensive midfield role, shackling the creative qualities of a player who thrived on inventive footwork and who possessed an ingenious knack of opening up attacking avenues that few other players could visualise. Not only were MSV constraining an undoubted talent and blind to the options they had at their disposal, they had created an unhappy and frustrated animal in Lubo and he was eager to wash his hands of the Duisburg contract.

Lubo had moved to Germany under the Jean Marc Bosman ruling and as he had cost Duisburg nothing, it was obvious a deal could be struck to prise this dejected midfielder away from a club who were mistakenly and unwisely using a silk shirt to clean the stairs.

Dr Jo was aware of his availability and he clearly knew of Lubo's capabilities but he was also learning fast and conscious of the fact that any moves for the player may well be greeted with ridicule in the press. The manager deliberated long and hard on the subject and again watched the player take to the field for Slovakia against Portugal in Bratislava.

Once more Lubo confirmed his fitness and a stamina belying his 33 years and although any move for the player couldn't be considered as a long-term solution to Celtic's problems, Dr Jo decided to face the wrath of fans and media alike by approaching Lubo. It didn't take Lubo long to weight up his options so the paperwork was set in motion with Duisburg for the midfielder to become the first ever Slovakian player to sign for Celtic.

"Obviously I'd heard about Celtic," he said "because I played for St Etienne before and I knew from their history they played against Celtic in the 1960s when Celtic were one of the biggest clubs in European football. But when I first came here I never really realised just how big a club Celtic actually were because I never had the chance to come here or play against Celtic. But I had always heard of the competition between Celtic and Rangers but when I was playing over in France in the 1990s, Rangers were dominating the Scottish scene and we really didn't hear much about Celtic."

That competition wasn't restricted to the field and Lubo's signing attracted the press reaction that Dr Jo had feared. 'Jozef's Boy' was one such headline as scorn was poured upon Celtic's latest acquisition and the penny-pinching attitude of their transfer limitations.

In the past Jock Stein, Ronnie Simpson, Pat Stanton and Billy Stark had all arrived at the club on the wrong side of 30 and while all four would eventually prove to be crucial signings, there was no great press reaction at the time. This was mainly due to the fact that no great expectations were heaped upon those earlier signings but in 1998 Celtic were in no position to make cosmetic peripheral signings and hope for the best. They had to get it right and Dr Jo was clearly taking a big gamble.

Any new signing had to be seen as a saviour. But redeemers cost a lot more than £300,000 and they were generally quite a bit younger than 33. Rangers had signed Scotland defender Colin Hendry who, at the same age as Lubo and with half as many international caps, cost a reported £4million. The comparisons weighed heavily in favour of the Ibrox man and he inadvertently was brought in to the equation as Celtic seemingly lost another battle in the tabloid war.

Hendry's age wasn't questioned to the same degree and the transfer fee was paraded as Rangers' purposeful willingness to part with big money to strengthen their squad. As we were soon to find out though, Celtic HAD unearthed a bargain and spent the paltry sum of £300,000 not on a 33-year-old bag of aching limbs and bones, but a 33-year-old football brain imbued with dexterity, technique and ability that had few equals in Europe. He had to be right for the team though and one good apple doesn't automatically turn everything in the basket rosy, Lubo had joined a new club and he had to get on with the normality of fitting in with his new team-mates.

"I knew a couple of the players like Henrik Larsson," he said "because I saw him play in the World Cup a couple of years before and Stephane Mahe obviously because I had played against him in France and I'd heard about a couple of the other players but I hadn't seen the team play. I didn't have time to think about how far the team was from the finished product because of everything that was happening. I had a chance to go to Japan but their offer was refused by Duisburg, then came Celtic and I thought this could be a real possibility."

The proof of the pudding is in the eating though and Lubo had yet to perform on the stage at Celtic Park and was as yet still an unknown quantity to the 58,093 fans who rolled up to the stadium on November 7. In the run-up to the Lubo signing Brown had told those in the know at Celtic that the wheels were in motion to sign this guy who had over 70 caps for his country, took all the free-kicks and corners and was the complete playmaker who rarely missed the target whether that be the goal or an on-running team-mate.

On face value this mystery signing seemed an exciting prospect but at the same time there was still a lingering doubt as they recalled similar enthusiasm from the GM on an earlier occasion. Previously he had clandestinely revealed to the chosen few that Celtic were on the verge of signing a player who would be a revelation and that the fans would go crazy for him. He was absolutely spot on, the fans did go crazy as the player in question was Regi Blinker.

So seeing is believing but there was irony in that Brown didn't see Lubo's debut for the Hoops. The GM and the club parted company on the morning of Lubo's first game against Dundee and it would seem that a depression was lifted from Celtic Park in one fell swoop as Lubo inspired Celtic to a 6-1 destruction of the Dens Park side.

The stadium was in buoyant mood as Lubo set up goals for Mark Burchill and Henrik Larsson before leaving the field after 70 min-

utes to a standing ovation. Jock Brown was no longer there to be ridiculed by the press and the scribes were realising that there was indeed something magical about this 30-something player from the bargain bin of European football.
The acid test was yet to come though and a fortnight later Rangers were to visit Celtic Park with a 10-point cushion and Celtic were seemingly lambs to the slaughter.

In the intervening weekend, Celtic had lost 2-1 away to St Johnstone so the euphoria over Brown's departure and the trouncing of Dundee may have been a one-off – or was it?
Old Firm games are by their very nature not occasions for the feint hearted and completely alien to many people in Scotland never mind those from foreign shores.

The divide, whether that be political, cultural, religious or just plain good old fashioned football preferences has to be witnessed to be even remotely understood as thousands of fans steadfastly stand behind their chosen team with a love and fervour for the club that is challenged only by their antipathy for those on the other side. Despite Lubo coming from a country that had split politically into Slovakia and the Czech Republic respectively, nothing prepared him for what lay in store.

"That parting of the ways in Czechoslovakia was a very crucial moment in my international career," said Lubo "because I was 28 and really at the peak of my football when I lost contact with the best of international football. When we split with the Czech Republic there were only two regular Slovakian players in Czechoslovakian team so we went through a very difficult period. We basically had to start from scratch and build everything from nothing because with just two experienced internationalist players things were going to be hard for us.

" But was there anything like the Old Firm back home? I don't think so, no because honestly, when we went to Ibrox and won 2-0 the first Old Firm game this season, I read Ronald De Boer saying in the matchday programme that even Barcelona and Real Madrid doesn't compare to the Old Firm rivalry. Nothing can compare to Celtic and Rangers honestly. In Prague maybe before the split there was Sparta and Slavia but it wasn't as big a derby as the Old Firm, there is nothing like it in Europe.

"Nothing prepared me for it especially as in Slovakia I played for Nitra which was a small club in small town and they had no great rivals of importance in football."

He added: "I don't really recall the press build up before the game because as I said already I was preparing for my first derby without reading the papers as I had only been here two weeks at the time. I couldn't really follow what was happening before the game in the newspapers but during the game and after it was absolutely fantastic. The cacophony of noise when we took to the pitch was absolutely brilliant. The atmosphere was incredible and something which I had never experienced before."

It wasn't only Lubo who was experiencing something for the first time as only those aged at least 45 and over would have had any worthwhile memories of the last time Celtic hit FIVE goals against their greatest rivals. Not since January 3, 1966 when "old man" Lubo was just five months old had Celtic so comprehensively torn apart their neighbours with a clinical, lethal and fruitful display and Lubomir Moravcik was the orchestrator of a divine 5-1 symphony that was to be christened the Demolition Derby.

Lubo scored the first two, was instrumental in much of the creative play on the day and even if the press had their initial doubts as to his capabilities, Rangers manager Dick Advocaat and his rearguard didn't as Scott Wilson was red carded for a reckless challenge on the Slovak. It was truly one of the most masterful Old Firm debuts ever but while Celtic Park erupted in sheer joy and exhilaration at both of Lubo's goals, he celebrated each of them with a mere shrug of the shoulders – he had nothing to prove and he knew it, the rest of us could only wonder where he had been all our lives.

"That game was fantastic, unbelievable but I have always truly felt that football has three basic elements and I have based my career on these three. They are talent, good health and third it's luck. Luck was a major ingredient that day and in football you definitely need luck. Without that you can't really realise your dreams. I think I had talent before the 5-1 game, I was ready physically and I was lucky. If everything comes together then it is something fantastic, something magical. I feel that during my whole career with Celtic except for the odd bad game I have had luck on my side.

"Even under Barnes and Dalglish the collective plan was bad, but then personally for me I extended my contract and I have to say I was lucky. But you can get good luck when you've got quality and you work hard for it. You can make your own luck. After this game I was accepted by the Celtic fans and it was good for me and for the future. That was a crucial moment for me and for Celtic. It was the turning point and the real beginning of my career here just two weeks after joining. It was a good start for me.

"I didn't feel anything bad against the press. You could say their reaction when I arrived was normal as I had never played in England or Scotland. For the previous five or six years had never played in the European Cup or World Cup and I was 33-years-old so their doubt about me was to be expected.

"At that time Celtic were 10 points behind Rangers and Dr Venglos brought me over. After the game Dr Venglos I remember said to me I helped him as well. He thought he helped me by signing me for Celtic and after this game I helped him by paying back for his faith in me. Dr Venglos was attacked in the press when he first arrived and now things were turning around for him."

Rangers were to have the last laugh though by winning the title and defeating Celtic in the Scottish Cup final on the last day of the season.

"I felt a little bit unlucky," said Lubo, "because I picked up an injury at a time when Celtic were really playing well and I stopped being an important part of the team. Unfortunately I couldn't play after three months and I came back to the team just before the cup final but I think I missed a little bit of form."

Amazingly, this exceptional talent had yet to win a medal in Celtic's colours, or the colours of any other team for that matter. That was to be put right the following season.

Through the eyes of coach Jozef Venglos

"I don't think we've yet fully appreciated his exceptional qualities as a player."

I'm familiar with Lubo's development as a footballer in almost every detail. When I took over the Czechoslovakian team he had played, if I remember correctly, only one game. After my first experience of coaching him, I found he had the qualities that our football was missing most. His strength is in the balance between his technical and tactical abilities and his individual ball skills, his ability to read the game and his imagination. Even as a young player he wasn't afraid of taking on responsibility.

This means that he's mentally very strong. He was already a key player at Nitra and eventually he became a key figure in the Czechoslovakia team. In my time as national coach, he played every game, in all the qualifiers and eventually at the 1990 World Cup in Italy. He brought skills to the team and he was also good at helping to create a relaxed and friendly atmosphere in the team. He was a ball player, he could hold on to the ball but he also recognised the right moment to pass it. His other strengths are his feel for the game and ability to change the rhythm of the play.

I still remember our debates about how, given his other excellent skills, he had to improve his defensive play. He certainly isn't the type to play a grafting role, he's a creative player, but he was asked to handle more of the defensive tasks. He managed to do that and became a much more valuable player to the team, and later he demonstrated his abilities by playing in the demanding French and Scottish leagues.

We have a good relationship as coach and player but I also see myself as his older friend. We've always been able to get on well, and working together at Celtic we became even closer.

Looking back as a coach, I see the significance of Czechoslovakia's last warm-up game just before the 1990 World Cup. We played Germany and lost 2-–1. At that time we had a surplus of left-footed players in the team, people like Knoflicek, Bilek, Kubik and Moravcik. After the game I realised that something had to be done about this, even at that late stage. I asked Lubo and Ivan Hasek to see me and explained the situation. I asked Ivan to play as a right attacking defender with Lubo in front of him, slightly off to the centre, and I tried to prepare them for it. They were both quite surprised and expressed their doubts.

The coach has to talk to players as well as to the whole team, so we discussed it and were able to clear all doubts between us. It was only a short time before we had to play our first World Cup match, against the USA. The switch worked beautifully – we probably surprised the Americans because they were expecting a different line-up, but now both sides of the team were equally strong.

What this experience confirmed to me is that it is good fortune if a coach can rely on intelligent footballers who can think and assess their position in the team and adjust accordingly to different demands. Both Hasek and Moravcik were players who not only fulfilled the coach's demands, but developed them further. This, to me, is the best mode of co-operation. The days when situations like that were dealt with by orders are gone.

I later followed the development of his football career. His qualities as a footballer opened up the opportunity of playing in France, and he became known throughout Europe. After my appointment as coach of Slovakia, he was the first player I picked and I also made him the captain. I based the Slovakian team I was building around Moravcik and Peter Dubovsky.

I came to Celtic only a few days before the start of the new season.

Fourteen Celtic players had been involved in the 1998 World Cup in France and I was getting to know the new environment and the players, many of whom hadn't had a break that summer. We also had some injuries, we had to bring in reinforcements, but we also had to get results. I recognised that the team needed a creative player.

Then I remembered Lubo, although I knew it would be a sensitive issue. I never doubted his qualities, his technical skills, which were more developed than those of the Scottish players, and I was certain he would be a great addition to the team.

This was later confirmed, but initially, when I announced that I wanted him, I had problems. The club management wasn't too hard to convince but inevitably some explanations were needed. My view was that his inclusion in the team would help the younger players who could learn from his skill and experience.

This was just one of the reasons justifying why I wanted to bring in a 33-year-old player. I had made my decision and wasn't going to budge but I was anxious about how it would be taken by the people around me and, more importantly, by the public.

I expected the media, especially the tabloids, to subject me to criticism. There were mocking headlines about the old man pushing his son into the club, bringing his protégé to Celtic and so on.

I ignored the invective and stood my ground. With the Celtic general manger, I went to see Lubo playing in an international match for Slovakia. Then, on the quiet, we made arrangements to finalise his move to Glasgow. There was another wave of ridicule.

Then came the match against Rangers. I put Lubo in the starting line-up and the papers were up in arms, asking why he and not the talented Mark Burchill was selected. It was a

long, long time since Celtic had beaten Rangers in the derby, but this time Celtic won 5–1. Lubo scored two goals and created two more with his passes. Now he was the supporters' favourite player and not just because he scored two goals – he enchanted them with the way he played and with his personality.

He deserved the standing ovation they gave him. The papers carried celebratory articles, praising him to the skies.

Fifty journalists turned up for the press conference. I managed to control myself and made only a little comment: "Gentlemen, I hope you were satisfied and realised that my protégé can play a bit. I don't want any apologies – I'm just happy we won."

The match was a turning point for him. Lubo won over the supporters and the media, but I recall another important moment. Before his first match, Lubo had trained only once with the team. Now, imagine the situation – in mid-season a new player comes to training for the first time, with every newspaper carrying negative comments about his arrival. The Celtic players were certainly very curious. We played a nine-a-side game at training. They could see the pleasure he took in playing, his fluent and easy running, dribbling, shooting with either foot, playing in standard situations, and they accepted him. He won the respect of all the players there and then, and he struck up an excellent striking partnership with Henrik Larsson.

Later, if a match was in the bag, I would substitute him so he could savour the ovation and the shouts of "Lubo! Lubo!" from the crowd. It was great. In the past he hadn't been so inclined to accept substitution. At the 1990 World Cup I replaced him towards the end of the match against the USA, when we were 5–1 ahead, and replaced him with Vlado Weiss. Lubo wasn't happy at all. "Lubo, we won, and Vlado had a game too – don't be so annoyed." I told him after the match. "But I wasn't the worst on the pitch," he said. "No, but it's not always the worst player who gets substituted," I tried to reassure him. He always wanted to stay on from the first minute to the last – and longer if possible!

Lubo is a good person. He just loves football. He's always played fairly, even though he's often been a target for opposition defenders. Sometimes he would argue over the referee's decisions, especially in the case of unsporting behaviour from an opposition player.

He became the biggest personality in Czechoslovakian and Slovakian football. At the moment he's the best-known Slovakian footballer playing abroad. I'm sorry that some of the differences between him and the Slovakian officials couldn't have been resolved so that they could have made use of his qualities in the Slovakian team. I don't think we've yet fully appreciated his exceptional qualities as a player.

Jozef Venglos, 65, formerly an outstanding footballer, was coach of Czechoslovakia (winning the 1976 European Championship with Vladimir Jezek and taking Czechoslovakia to two World Cups) and later became coach of Slovakia. He also coached many leading clubs at home and abroad, the last of which was Celtic. He is now a FIFA and UEFA expert. He was voted Slovakia's Coach of the Century.

THE DARKEST HOUR

Who is the best player you have ever played with?

"Henrik Larsson, he is just a fantastic player."

So Lubomir Moravick experienced his first end-of-season at Celtic Park and despite his vibrant displays there were no celebratory parties in Paradise as spring turned to summer in 1999. The Celts had finished second in the league just six points behind Rangers as the Old Firm recorded one win each and two draws against each other that past season.

In the League Cup there was an embarrassing 1-0 defeat at Airdrie as the pre-Moravcik Celts went out minus six first-team regulars and within minutes were saying goodbye to a trophy it had taken the club 15 years to win. Celtic did take care of Airdrie in the Scottish Cup and went all the way to the final only to be beaten 1-0 by Rangers but the Hoops fans had experienced worse seasons although at that time we didn't know what was lurking around the corner.

Europe was another wash-out after two ties in the Champions League qualifying rounds (St Patrick's Athletic and Croatia Zagreb) and another two in the UEFA Cup (Vitoria Guimaeres and FC Zurich) but the fans had long since expected anything but a short run in European football.

Lubo had taken part in 17 League and Scottish Cup games scoring six goals, Celtic's League Cup and European adventures were over by the time he arrived. On the first-team front Simon Donnelly, Phil O'Donnell, Darren Jackson, David Hannah, Malky Mackay, Brian McLaughlin and John Paul McBride had all departed as the reshaping of the team continued.

But it was the off-field departures that created the big news although Fergus McCann's leaving was planned and as expected as Jock Brown's wasn't. McCann had arrived like a million dollar hero in a five-and-ten-cents store in March 1994 with a five-year plan to turn Celtic around. He was a shrewd investor and the one thing he didn't promise was success on the field, such was his conviction everything else he promised was 'guaranteed.'

There was limited success on the pitch though as all three domestic trophies had been captured during his tenure including the face-saving Championship of Wim Jansen's residency to stop Rangers completing the unimaginable 10-in-a-row. Off the park, McCann had delivered but the lack of gleaming silver in the trophy room barely did justice to the massive strides the club had taken elsewhere.

Celtic were the nearly men of Scottish football and when that field in the eyes of many constitutes just two teams separated by a few miles of Glasgow streets in geographical terms but light years in terms of stature within the game then "nearly" is plainly not good enough.

The huge expectations had taken their toll and for the third season in a row Celtic were looking for a new manager – Dr Jozef Venglos had decided to hang up his managerial cap and allow someone else to take over the mantle that was increasingly becoming a poisoned chalice. It's no wonder that many hankered for the old days when there was a board of directors, mainly faceless businessmen headed by a chairman, and a manager who ruled the roost by the maxim of a place for everything and everything in its place.

But football was changing rapidly and Celtic in this respect at least were not being left behind in the corporate and administrative race. The three off-field departures had been Managing Director, Football General Manager and Head Coach. The replacements were designated as Chief Executive, Director of Football Operations and Head Coach. Only the latter retained the same title and after all what's in a name but the fans on the street were a bit bemused by all the labelling and still yearned to have a single "manager" at the head of the team.

Dr Jo still retained a satellite position within the club as European Technical Advisor and his remit was to scour the continent, paying specific attention to Eastern Europe, for up and coming talent in the hope of unearthing a new Lubo. But the 'old' Lubo was still here and far from wallowing in any self-pity about no longer working with his mentor, the Slovak was determined to stay and slog it out – if the new regime of John Barnes and Kenny Dalglish wanted him.

"Dr Venglos told me the offer was there for him to stay but that he didn't think he could last another year. He was tired and he was past 60 and it was a very hard season for him because at the beginning he arrived a little bit late and he didn't have the team that he wished. He arrived in a period when Mr McCann wasn't investing in the first team as much as a manager would like and so it was not an easy season for Dr Venglos.

"But if he had one regret it was the Scottish Cup final because I think he did a good job for Celtic and I feel he wanted to leave with a cup victory behind him. Unfortunately we didn't win. At that time Rangers were in the situation that we have been in recently. Dominating the game and playing with confidence and it's not easy to beat that sort of team. When the season was over I put the question to myself what will happen after Dr Venglos? He brought me here and this always happens in football when a new manager comes along but when I came back after a holiday I was talking to Barnes and he said if you stay it's no problem, I want you for the new season and I said it's no problem as I was happy with that."

McCann's departure had paved the way for Allan MacDonald to take over the reins of the club at the very top as Celtic approached the new millennium with renewed hope and optimism. MacDonald was a dyed in the wool Celtic supporter who had flew to the higher echelons of British Aerospace and was infused with a determination to make Celtic great again.

Such was the Chief Executive's resolve that he was willing to gamble on appointments but sadly the odds eventually proved to be too heavily backed against him and the men he fought to bring in. There had been the by now annual speculation as to who would take on the managerial job at Celtic and if Lubo was taking this in his stride he may have been wondering why everyone else was pulling their hair out at the thought of yet another managerless close season.

MacDonald was a friend and golfing partner of Kenny Dalglish and there was no doubt that in the eyes of many fans the former player was still a Celtic hero, a Scotland legend and one of the biggest names in football. In the early to mid 1970s he quite literally was Celtic and although the team were still winning trophies in the middle of the decade, if you took Dalglish and Danny McGrain from the side then you were left with a very ordinary team indeed.

That was the problem. Someone did take Dalglish from the side and in 1977 he moved south to Liverpool for £440,000, a fee that many felt was a bargain at the time and over the next few seasons they were proved to be absolutely correct. Dalglish went on to become a living legend at Anfield and managerial stints at Liverpool, Blackburn Rovers and Newcastle United proved relatively successful but costly.

Many doubted his prowess in the transfer market and the school of thought was that not only did he buy big for success, but that the triumphs rarely matched the outgoing fees spent on players and wages. There was also the underlying current among supporters who still hadn't forgiven Dalglish for leaving the club in 1977 and fans with long memories are short on patience.

And there was yet another surprise as Dalglish approached MacDonald with a short list of one for the managerial candidate. That man was John Barnes, another Liverpool legend who had also plied his trade on the world stage with the England national side and was admired on all four corners of the globe for his skill on the field, but he had never managed a team and the thought of anyone, even someone as respected as Barnes, serving his managerial apprenticeship with a club

of the stature of Celtic had many fans scratching their heads in disbelief.

Hope, optimism and the genuine desire for the new regime to succeed was tinged with pessimism, apprehension and the concern that Rangers were once again going to romp home with the title. Not only was Barnes a novice in the managerial stakes but Celtic were treading the water for the third year running with a new manager and for the third year in succession a manager that had no prior link with the club.

The latter point may seem a trifle trite but every other manager, bar Dublin-born Liam Brady who was a Celtic supporter and knew the club's expectations, had played for the team and more importantly were aware of the need to overcome Rangers above all else.

Dalglish himself knew the appointment was a gamble but Barnes said at the time: "My views on how the game should be played have already been passed on to the players and together I'm confident we can produce the winning formula. We are involved in what basically is a simple game but a little bit of reason and understanding can make it even simpler – and therefore more effective.

"The players here are intelligent men and experienced professionals and although we cannot put a time on when all aspects will gel, we know it will happen and the signs are hopeful that it will be sooner rather than later. The main aspect here is communication and I have the confidence in my own ability to make that function as easy as possible. This is not rocket science we are talking about but the attitude, commitment, professionalism and discipline of everyone here is very important."

Those words were spoken in the summer of 1999 and just seven months later in February 2000, the last line in particular was to have a very hollow ring to it, but in the meantime Celtic were heralding a new beginning and the mood in the camp at least was hopeful as the two big names took their first training sessions under their new moniker of the Celtic Dream Team.

"We were definitely hopeful at first," said Lubo, "When a new manager arrives I think it gives new hope for the fans and for the club, that's normal especially with guys like Dalglish and Barnes. When they took the job they did so in the good faith and with good intentions to do something positive."

But did the new management style suit the team and its aspirations? Even now Lubo can't pinpoint an exact answer and just as he himself states luck as one of the three vital factors in a successful football career, even the most cynical among us would concede that fate played a part in the eventual downfall of Barnes and Dalglish, with Henrik Larsson's horrific leg-break on European duty in Lyon on October 21 having a significant bearing on the proceedings.

"I don't know really. We started well and everything was okay but then you can't compensate for an injury to a guy like Henrik Larsson," recalled Lubo, "and that was a big negative for the team psychologically. That was a massively depressing moment for us. In football it is difficult to really analyse who was at fault and when the rot set in but after the winter break things didn't go well for us. Before that we were really close to Rangers but nothing really happened and we lost against Hearts in the league before the Inverness Caley Scottish Cup game changed everything."

With the advantage of hindsight the Inverness Caley game seemed like an accident just waiting to happen. On the morning of the original scheduled date of January 29 the Clyde was flowing high and fast. The water was choppy, brown, ugly and menacing and there was a terrible sense of foreboding. A piece of guttering above the Lisbon Lions' Stand had come loose in the near storm-like conditions. It was patently obvious that the game would be called off and sure enough eventually someone with the correct authority signalled that the game couldn't go ahead in the interests of public safety.

The tie was rescheduled for the midweek date of Tuesday, February 8 and on that night although the storm had long since subdued, it seemed the Clyde had burst its banks and deluged the hearts of every Celtic supporter in the city. An entirely different type of storm was looming in the dark winter night.

Inverness Caledonian Thistle to give them their Sunday name played the deadly role in what proved to be a calamitous season for Celtic. It wasn't the first time a major team had been knocked out of a cup by a side from a lower division but there were prevailing circumstances that made this even more of a debacle in the eyes of the public. The side is an amalgamation of two Inverness teams from the Highland League, a division which has always been considered a bit of a joke when it comes to the Scottish Cup. So, in effect, in the public eye the mighty Glasgow Celtic had been knocked out of the cup not by a team of fellow professionals.

But by part-time yokels who had just moved up from a Mickey Mouse league and who had only been in existence for less than six years. The visitors came in for the break 2-1 ahead and Celtic came out after the break minus star striker Mark Viduka. He had apparently refused to return for the second half after a shouting match in the dressing room. All hell broke loose and there was hell to pay in the aftermath to one of the most shocking displays ever by a team in the green and white hoops.

"At half time I didn't really understand everything," said Lubo, "because all this shouting was going on and everyone was speaking very fast. Maybe the mistake was in that at half time we tried to analyse what was happening. Looking back that was the biggest mistake. We should have relaxed and let one guy say something but everyone was shouting at once and sticking their tuppence worth in because we knew things were going wrong and the game wasn't working out well for us.

"What happened just got the team even more down and negative and in the second half we weren't able to turn the game around. We were really down mentally and I think the team missed having a player in the right frame of mind who could change the game because we were definitely bad that night."

He added: "I remember when I was playing with St Etienne right at the tail end of the season and we were down at the bottom of the table in real trouble. We dropped important points after being 3-1 ahead in the second last game of the season and the fans were waiting for us outside the ground after the game. That was exactly the same feeling as the Inverness Caley game. St Etienne were 3-1 ahead with two minutes to go and the game finished 3-3 to put us in a really bad position in the table but at the end of the season we didn't go down.

"But the people were very angry about it and this was the same situation. We couldn't leave the stadium after the game. This has happened twice in my life and it wasn't very pleasant at all and I didn't feel very good about being part of that."

In the aftermath of the 3-1 defeat Head Coach John Barnes, Assistant Head Coach Eric Black and Chief Scout/Coaching Assistant Terry McDermott all walked, Kenny Dalglish took over all first-team matters and the big inquest in to what was wrong at Celtic went on. In earlier happier times Barnes' initial league record was being compared to that of Jock Stein's when Celtic's greatest ever manager first took over the post but that was short-lived.

No matter how good the comparisons looked it must be said that Stein achieved his primary success with very little outlay in the purchase of players. The same could hardly be said of Barnes' spending policy and many questions were being asked of the quality of player he was bringing in. On a lighter note there was the famous incident against Hearts early on in the season when Lubo trapped the ball with his backside as Celtic romped to 4-0 win.

"I had already performed this trick back in my home country," he said, "sometimes inspiration comes and if the moment is right you go ahead and do it. But it is not something that should be done lightly and it's something I don't recommend making a habit of. You don't just do it for nothing and the circumstances have to be right. If you do it once then everyone will remember and that is all you need – although maybe I will do it in my last game for Celtic.

"Sometimes things like that come off but in football it's first things first and winning the game is the most important thing. I wouldn't have done it if we had been drawing 0-0 at the time but honestly football is not a circus, it is a serious job."

Life carried on after the Inverness Caley debacle and a couple of weeks later Celtic fans were overjoyed when Lubo decided to sign another contract with the club when there were fears that he would be returning to France in a coaching capacity. He was offered a similar coaching role with Celtic but in the end opted to concentrate solely on the playing side and that was one crumb of comfort the Bhoys faithful had in a season that was rapidly disintegrating before their very eyes.

There was the League Cup to fight for though and just a week after the Inverness Caley catastrophe, Celtic earned the right to contest the final thanks to a solitary goal from Lubo in the semi-final at Hampden against Kilmarnock.

Aberdeen provided the opposition in the final and goals from Vidar Riseth and Tommy Johnson gave Celtic the win they so badly needed but Dalglish refused to take any plaudits for the trophy win. He said it was Barnes' team that got to the final and Barnes' team that won it but the win did throw up an amazing fact in the eyes of the Celtic support. This was Lubo's first ever winners' medal and after watching him perform miracles for a year-and-a-half the fans were convinced that this magician must have a drawer full of medals at home.

"In my honest opinion," he said, "I think in football there are plenty of good players who have never won a medal because not every good player is surrounded by footballers of similar quality. It is important to be happy within yourself and I was always happy with my career, it's not finished yet and although there is less than one season left I will honestly do my best for Celtic before I leave.

"I never like to say never but I'm convinced this is my last season and it would be great to repeat the Treble we won last season as well as making a name for ourselves by gaining a reputation in the Champions League. As for the determination to win more, you never know what is going to happen later on."

So Lubo had collected his first ever winners' medal but would it also be his last?

LIFE IN SCOTLAND

What is the best goal you have ever scored?

"I think my first goal for the national team. It was against Switzerland in the World Cup qualifications and it was an important goal for me. The best goal I have ever scored for Celtic was my first against Rangers."

To quote Robert Burns; "O wad some Power the giftie gie us, To see oursels as ithers see us!" Maybe it's a Scottish trait but we always seem to wonder why anyone in their right mind would want to come here when the vast majority of the population constantly dream of a place in the sun.

In footballing terms the argument is that clubs can pay big bucks to any player willing to ply his trade here but there are bigger and better bucks not to mention far more attractive lifestyles elsewhere yet we can appeal to footballers from all over the globe. It's something that never fails to amaze some Scots although our bigger cities are now far more cosmopolitan than they have ever been. Indian, Italian and Chinese restaurants have always been part of the Glaswegian dietary needs but these days you can opt for French, Russian, Thai or any number of national dishes from the global menu.

But try finding a Scottish restaurant in Paris or Vienna, in fact try finding a Scottish eatery in Argyll Street and you'll be hard pushed. We just don't have that sort of image and the world can be eternally grateful that the pizza base was invented in Italy, if it had been a Scottish creation then the toppings would be mouth-watering delicacies such as turnip and cabbage.

It doesn't work does it? We definitely have some beautiful scenery and on the face of it are a friendly old bunch but in the dreamworld of most Scots they would opt for the left bank of the Seine and the French Riviera to the Gallowgate and Saltcoats any day.

Even many of those who are Glaswegian to the core would agree that the grass is always greener on the other side and when it comes to comparing our climate and lifestyle to that of our European cousins it would appear to most that our glass is half empty rather than half full.

That is what we are up against when we try to tempt players to our freezing shores and the clubs have to pull out all the stops to convince any potential newcomers. It's obvious that even here players live in an elevated lifestyle with a more than decent income, plenty of time off and they reside in the better parts of the city, but even life in the Premiership down south must seem much more appealing than bringing the wife and weans to the Central Belt for a couple of years.

But foreign players are a way of life in Scottish football now and we must take pride in the fact that we can attract players from all manner of nationalities to our game. The Old Firm obviously have the upper hand in this and not only because they are known throughout the world, have massive supports and can offer big money.

They can present an all-round more attractive and sexier package than other teams who are trying to compete with them even though outside in the real world it's still Scotland. Picture the scene, a new arrival turns up at Celtic Park for signing talks and right away he is encapsulated by the wonderful all-seated, all-covered stadium that attracts 60,000 people every other week. Inside the stadium he views the many restaurants and lounges, is shown the club's glossy magazine, the website, the superstore and all the other trappings an operation the size of Celtic entails. He thinks, 'this is the very dab, just the thing for me.' And signs on the dotted line and then makes his debut in the League Cup on a wet Tuesday night at Falkirk!

The other side of the coin doesn't sound very glamorous but for whatever reason we do pull in many players from abroad and Lubo Moravcik is just one of the many who are now here but football according to him is a trade like any other and he had no trepidation about uprooting wife Susanna and kids Matus (13) and Roberta (9) and bringing them to Scotland after living in France.

"That wasn't really a problem for me," he said, "because I had already left my home country nine years beforehand and when the opportunity arrived to come to Scotland I took it.
"Not even the weather put me off because football is my job and I didn't come here for a holiday, I came for football but obviously in the background what I was looking for was to find schooling for my children.

"This was literally my fear and I was trying to find a French-speaking school but later on I found the solution for my children because they did the translations at home and did English at school. They have really settled in now but not immediately because at first I didn't know about their school programme but by my second season with Celtic they came and settled very quickly.

"Obviously everyone knows that I'm their father as that is life but they are going to school to learn so they just get on with it and yes the kids have Scottish accents now. They are learning the language in schools and on the street with their friends so they pick things up quicker and they obviously have Scottish accents. Matus is playing for Celtic Boys' Club at under-13 level and he's getting on okay and very happy to be involved with the side.

"He plays right midfield and he takes after me but when I was younger I played on the left side of midfield that is the only difference. I get along and participate in the training sessions whenever I can and it's a pleasure for me to be involved. I can't be there all the time because of my first-team commitments but I know what it's like for the youngsters when I am there.

"I can remember when I was young and the contact we had with first-team players as it was always an exciting moment and it's important to keep a close association with the youngsters coming through the system. This sort of contact is vital and when I was younger I was in the same awe of the big players and it's always going to be like that."

That's the kids taken care of but because of the Old Firm celebrity status, footballers in Glasgow lead pretty much a goldfish-bowl style of existence which can cause problems for a stranger in a strange land with plenty of time on his hands.

"I have my programme," said Lubo, "where I train in the morning and then there is my free time in the afternoon but the difficulty here is that the time the children have off doesn't always coincide with mine. When the children were younger it was easier to take off in the afternoon and go visiting places but now of course they are at school in the afternoon.

"Even if I have a day off I can't make too many plans as I have to go and pick the children up from school. It's not very often now that we get a free day at the weekend but if that happens and Matus is playing then I can get along and see the game but that is very rare. We try to go to the cinema or maybe 10-pin bowling, these are really the only activities that we can do together as a family.

"To relax away from football I do just that – relax and do nothing special. I rest a lot, I come home and watch TV, I like to watch football. I've read about a lot of players who say they don't want to watch football because they work in the game everyday. But I will watch football at any time, even under-17 or whatever level because I have the spare time and I don't have a big circle of friends.

"I know now that also at my age I need a lot of rest to recover after training and to be ready for the next day. I have to keep my energy for the training because at my age the recovery time is different and it can be more difficult. I watch movies on the video and listen to music but being in a foreign country I don't really spend too much time out of my own house so much of the time is spent staying in and relaxing.

"Honestly, I have to mention that it can be a little bit boring because every day is really similar, even at the weekend because I don't have family here and can't really see my friends. But it is a sacrifice that is worth it to play for a club like Celtic. I could go back to Slovakia to play but then I wouldn't be playing for a big club like Celtic. You know we can't have everything. I can't play for Celtic AND be in Slovakia with my friends so I sacrifice some social life for the football life.

"I profit from it though as the most important thing for me is football and hopefully I will still have time after football to catch up. I listen to a lot of Slovakian music, pop and folk music as when I'm feeling a little bit down I need some nostalgic music. Slovakian music from when I was younger because I love my country and I miss my country so the music helps.

"I have Slovakian books and videos sent over but generally when I finish training I don't go home. I go into the city about three times a week to an Italian restaurant and read Slovakian magazines and after I do the crosswords I leave to go and pick the kids up from school. This is mostly my daily routine.

"I can relax quietly in the restaurant because by the time I get home with the kids it is always a little bit noisy. I can honestly say it's not easy to be a footballer when your children are that little bit older because they also have their own activities. When they were smaller it was easier and if I had my family around to child-mind it would be easier but arranging your time to suit the kids is just one of the joys of parenthood!"

There are the occasional visits from his family back home in Slovakia but these are few and far between so Lubo much prefers the close season break when he can return to his homeland.

"Yes, my mother comes over sometimes, but the problem is that there are no direct flights and my mother doesn't speak English and she isn't so confident about changing flights in London so it is not so easy to organise especially as you need a visa. Sometimes there is a problem getting a visa even though I am working here. But even when my mother comes over here it can be boring for her because of the language problem and she doesn't drive so they are happier when I visit them over in Slovakia.

"Even to sit and watch Slovakian TV in the evenings and catch up on things with friends and family back home when I go back is a joy."

Lubo fully understands his mother's difficulty with the language and despite Slovakian being his mother tongue and living in an English-speaking country he admits that he still thinks in French. And when he first arrived at Celtic he was ever so slightly dependent on French speakers like Stephane Mahe and Eric Black who had finished off his playing career in France with Metz.

"Yes I was a bit closer to the French speakers when I first arrived, this was a great help and very positive for me when I first arrived here. Firstly, Dr Venglos could obviously talk

away to me in Slovakian and also Eric helped me a lot to settle in domestically as well as in the dressing room and on the training ground."

To this day there is still a French impression on his day-to-day life at Celtic as his closest friend is Didier Agathe whose mother tongue is also French.

"Didier Agathe is my closest friend here," he said, "as we room together when the team are away. Didier is a French speaker and that is a big help, for Didier as well as me. But he is a great guy to room with as if I want to read for example, he has no problem with the light being on or if I want to watch TV it is no big thing with him. He is a quiet guy and I get on great with him, it's a good partnership and that is important because we are staying in hotels quite a lot these days."

He added: "I still think in French as I watch a lot of French TV and so it is now really natural for me and I don't even translate things now as I pick things up in French. English I still have to translate in my head and even now I am not too quick at that. I'm not quick enough to automatically translate English but even though as a Slovak I don't speak French like a native, it is no problem for me."

And as for the notorious Glasgow accent? ***"Of course it always takes some time to understand people when they have got a strong accent," he laughed, "because I was learning from a book and what I read in the book was different from what I was hearing!"***

Lubo isn't the only Slovakian national performing in the Scottish Premier League at the moment and he has forged a friendly relationship with Robert Tomaschek at Hearts.

"He is from my home town," said Lubo, "and he started at the same club as me in Nitra. We socialise together but it is not easy as he also has a family and even though he is not far away it is still a 45-

minute drive. As for me giving him advice when he first came here, I didn't really know him that well before he arrived over here. We both played for the national team but he is not of my generation. When you turn up for the national team you naturally tend to split into different age groups and I spent most of my time with players of my own age and he is about seven years younger than me.

"So at that time I didn't know him too well but obviously now I know him much better and our families get together on occasion. Our home town of Nitra is a very small city of about 100,000 people and we usually travel back there with both families together."

Although Tomaschek must value the comradeship of a fellow Slovak in a strange land he maybe looks forward to these family get-togethers and plane trips with a bit of trepidation as Lubo seems to have the Indian Sign over Hearts and has a healthy habit of scoring against them.

"He is happy when I am not playing against Hearts," laughed Lubo, "he says if I play then I am almost surely going to score. He was very, very lucky, no only kidding, just lucky that in his first game for Hearts against Celtic they won 3-2 and it was a really bad time for us."
It's obvious from his performances on the park that Lubo is a bit of a perfectionist in his training regime and practising his skills.

His fitness routine is also followed to the utmost degree and he is so fanatical about his health and condition that he is considering taking up vegetarianism when he gives up the playing side of the game. But there are two other areas of his professional life where he is even more pernickety and a bit of a regular fusspot. One of his peculiarities means slightly less work for the boot boys on the groundstaff at Celtic Park while the other is nothing but a pain in the neck to Celtic kit man John Clark.

The first involves Lubo being a bit of a mechanic when it comes to boots and their studs and he doesn't trust anyone with his beloved boots.

"This habit stems from my beginnings in football," he said, "When I started, football wasn't like now. I'm not THAT old but 25 years ago when I started picking up the game as a kid things were different back home and we couldn't buy Adidas or Puma because at this period one brand dominated in Slovakia and our boots were very simple and basic.

"But later when I got my first real boots made of leather when I was 14-years-old I was looking after them every day, I polished them every day – I slept with them That was about 20 years ago and I was a bit of a maniac with them, taking them to bed with me and this habit I have now came from then.

"When you start to look after your boots you don't want anyone else to look after them. They are the tools of my trade and even now I like them to be polished perfectly. I don't want to see any marks on them and every small area gets the same perfect treatment. It's a bit of a mania with me but I am always looking after my boots, honestly it is my passion. Also. What I wear is very important for me, and my entire strip has to be perfect as well – it's my job.

"I even like my socks to be perfect. I know that once the game starts I don't have much control over my kit and can't keep it clean but when I go on to the pitch I have got too feel right. After that I don't really care once I am on the pitch but it is NOT a superstition, it is an obsession. Ask Clarky about it, sometimes I am very fussy and I am always getting on at him when things aren't exactly right. I say I don't want these socks as they aren't perfect so I think I am his most difficult customer.

"Before I became professional, football was my passion and it still is my passion now that I am professional. It has stayed my passion and so my habit hasn't changed from then until now. But it's a pleasure because you know it doesn't take a long time to polish you boots and make things right."

THE TREBLE

Who was your football hero as a young boy?

"First, when I was really young it was Kevin Keegan, after that it was Platini."

Another season had ended albeit a traumatic one for Celtic and their supporters but Lubo Moravcik after years of performing fantastically for several clubs and two national teams had finally won his first ever winners' medal.

In the grand scheme of things though the League Cup is the least laudable of all three domestic trophies. No longer is there an automatic European place at stake and the competition has declined in stature down through the years. Everybody wants to win it but there is no real wailing and gnashing of teeth if either of the Old Firm get knocked out unless it is by the other half of the Glasgow dynasty.

Compare the reaction to Celtic being knocked out of the Scottish Cup by Inverness Caley to their prior displacement by Airdrie in the previous season's League Cup.
Night and day would be the obvious contrast and if the truth be known the real appeal of the competition is that a Treble is harder to win than a Double and thereby lies the actual value of the trophy.

The Glasgow Cup initially was a treasured prize and gradually went to seed down through the decades. The big two were progressively utilising reserve players in the tournament until it lost its magic for the supporters and it is now purely a youth team competition, but in its heyday it was a significant part of the football calendar drawing massive crowds and when Celtic swept the boards in 1966/67 by winning the League Cup, the Scottish Cup, the League Championship, the European Cup AND the Glasgow Cup it just wouldn't have been the same if Rangers or any of the other Glasgow sides had secured the now comparatively meaningless trophy.

The League Cup is in severe danger of following the same slippery slope as its Glasgow counterpart but you can't win the Treble without it. The problem was that when Celtic won the League Cup in the Barnes/Dalglish season all they confirmed was that no team would win the Treble that year, Celtic had already been stuffed in the Scottish Cup and were so far behind Rangers in the Championship race, the table made for embarrassing reading.

At the end of the day Celtic trailed Rangers by a massive 21-point deficit and the long and winding road to the end of the season only delayed what seemed inevitable when Kenny Dalglish and Celtic parted company once more. For the fourth season in a row Celtic were looking for a manager once more and the board pulled out all the stops to get it right this time.

Martin O'Neill had worked wonders at Leicester City so there were no quibbles about his qualifications for the job and his Celtic background in Ireland was tailor-made for the vagaries and demands of tugging the reins at Kerrydale Street. For once everyone seemed to be in accord. The press, the fans and more importantly the players but would it work, would it be another false dawn? We would soon find out.

When a manager arrives at a new club it's reasonable to take a leap in logic here and assume that the first thing he would do is appraise the squad he has at his disposal. Taking into consideration the stature and standing of the club, the expectations of the club and the fans and the budget available to him he would presumably evaluate each individual player and ask himself the question, 'If he wasn't here already would I buy him?'

Similarly, every player at a club with an incoming manager must lose sleep at night wondering if the new man will rate him although over the previous three terms the Celtic squad regulars were becoming seasoned professionals at dealing with this predicament. But if Martin O'Neill was indeed assessing his new squad knowing that, if the previous season was anything to go by, he would have to clear out a lot of deadwood, would there be any place at all for a 35-year-old who had been toying with retirement for the last couple of seasons?

However, as far as Lubo Moravcik was concerned he wasn't a 35-year-old trying to prove himself, he was simply a footballer trying to prove himself and that was something he had done ever since he first kicked a football as a kid.

"In football this is never finished," he said, "even if you are in the team and you win one day you have to win another day. You can't say I'm 27 so it will be okay, it's not done, it's never done, even at 35 it's not done. I know what I can do but it's just a question of getting the chance and before you get that chance you have to show that you want it, you have to fight for it.

"I knew the position I wanted and I was prepared to battle for it, I didn't want to play anywhere else and when I got the role, that is when I had to show my character. My character means I am the type of player who wants to do his best right now, not six months down the line. I don't have to be number one because that is not always easy but I have to be ready and available to do my bit when I am called upon.

"When I do my job I try to do my best even if that is only for the last 15 minutes of a game. And that is to the end, not because I am now 36-years-old, I have always approached the game that way. I don't have that 'I don't care' approach. Why do stupid things now when I am in the final months of my playing career, when I didn't do that before? When I was 18 or 19-years-old I used to say why be stupid and now I want to finish my career in the best possible way by maintaining that same attitude and those same standards of self motivation.

"It's not easy, maybe I won't play anymore but I will do my best to get this chance. If I don't get it because there are a lot of good players around then so be it and at 36 I can't be sure there isn't a guy aged 22 with international caps staking a better claim than me for a first-team place. I don't want to be compared to anyone but I want to do MY best and that is all I can drive myself towards. If I do my best and there is someone better than me then that is okay but at least I will know I have given 100 per cent.

"It is important for me within myself to give my all and train and perform to the best of my abilities. If my best means only three games in a season or every single game then at least I know it has been total commitment, that is all I can ask of myself and that is all a coach can ask of a player."

Moravcik was indeed part of O'Neill's plans as the Celts opened the season at a canter and after six straight wins came the first real test of the season when Rangers came to Parkhead on August 27, 2000 for one of the most eagerly anticipated Old Firm games in years. The fans had barely settled in their seats before Chris Sutton fired Celtic ahead

and the goals just seemed to keep on coming as with little more than 20 minutes on the clock the Bhoys were three in front and firing on all cylinders.

The Celts weren't finished there though and Sutton finished the game the way he started by knocking in the sixth Celtic goal of a totally breathtaking 90 minutes. Henrik Larsson also hit a double, one of them just about the sweetest goal you are ever likely to see and Stilian Petrov got the other. Celtic won 6-2 and this was the big one - the first real sign that things were changing positively and Lubo had played a vital role in yet another historic game against Rangers.

"That was a very important game for everyone," he said, "and I can compare the 6-2 game to my first match against Rangers when we won 5-1. Because that first game was important for me and it was important for Dr Venglos just as the 6-2 game was important for Martin and for the new group.

"It wasn't so much an absolutely new group as there were still some players from the 5-1 match in the team but it was a new situation. Just as our first Old Firm game this season which we won 2-0 was important, obviously it's better when you have a good start even when you don't know how the season is going to end. I mean I got off to a good start against Rangers in my first game but the league didn't work out for us that season. But it's obviously better to have a good start rather than a bad one and keep that going in a positive manner rather than a negative one trying to catch up on a difficult situation. It is better to look back at the other teams than run after them"

The rollercoaster surged on and almost exactly three months later when Celtic travelled to Ibrox for the next Old Firm clash they had still to taste their first domestic defeat of Martin O'Neill's reign. However, that afternoon proved to be the first blot on the landscape as a lacklustre Celtic side amazingly suffered a 5-1 defeat.

"You know, it's difficult to analyse what happened that day," said Lubo, "but the important thing is how a team reacts to something like that and a good team's reaction is positive. I remember in the Barnes/Dalglish season Hearts beat us 3-2 at a very crucial time then came the Inverness Caley game a few days later and that just arrived too soon so we didn't play the way we wanted but our reaction after that was negative.

"But following the 5-1 defeat our response was positive even though we had another top-of-the-table clash with Hibs the following week. We had a hard-fought 0-0 draw with a very good Hibs side and built on that again by going on a winning streak to keep the bandwagon rolling."

That first blot on the landscape turned out to be the only such black mark as the Celts rallied and outwardly at least carried on as if the 5-1 defeat had never happened. Win after win kept rolling in with the odd draw here and there proving only to be minor irritations on the march to glory. The first couple of hurdles in the much-maligned League Cup had been safely negotiated but the semi-final threw up old adversaries Rangers.

Another double from Larsson, including a sublime chip and a counter from Sutton helped Celtic to a 3-1 win at Hampden on February 7, 2001, almost exactly a year to the day of the Inverness Caley embarrassment. But the game was all but over when another big talking point arrived in the final minute.
An altercation on the by-line resulted in FOUR red cards and one of them was for Lubo after Rangers' Claudio Reyna took out both Bobby Petta and Paul Lambert. It was diabolical tackle and Lubo got involved with Michael Mols so both received red cards to add to the TWO shown at Reyna.

"It was one game and I was a little bit stupid," recalled Lubo, "even in Slovakia and France I wasn't known as a 'bad boy' but sometimes when I feel an injustice has been done I

want to see it righted and in a stupid moment I questioned a bad tackle. Then he pushed me and we pushed each other. Sometimes it's yellow, sometimes it's red and you take it in the context of the game. I wasn't unlucky, I was stupid and I can't change that, it's all in the past."

Just four days later the Old Firm were in action against each other again this time on league duty and a solitary Alan Thompson goal marked the sea change in Glasgow's superiority stakes as Celtic again took all three points. The points tally just kept on clocking up and both Dunfermline and Hearts were disposed of in the Scottish Cup before the League Cup final came around on March 18, 2001 as Celtic maintained their bid to retain the trophy and Lubo wondered if he was going to collect his second winners' medal.

He did indeed play in the final as a Larsson hat-trick was scored with no reply by Kilmarnock and Lubo now had a matching pair of League Cup winners' medals but did he think the Treble was on or did he have any fears?

"No. You dream," he said, "you say maybe we can do the other two. Okay we are in a good situation in the league here, almost comfortable and definitely favourites for the title but by the time you come to the Scottish Cup final you realise it's a one-off game and you never know what will happen.

"I said to myself though, we've got a chance as we've worked hard to get this far. It's very difficult though because you can dream all you want but you have to fight to get the chance to make those dreams come true. But for Celtic that chance was a reality. We could try to do it, we were the only team that could do it."

With the League Cup safely tucked away in the trophy cabinet results elsewhere meant it didn't take Einstein to work out that victories in Celtic's next three league games, all played within one calendar week, would have the SPL trophy nestling neatly alongside it.

Celtic beat Aberdeen 1-0 with Lubo's room-mate Didier Agathe scoring the all-important goal on April 1 at Pittodrie, on April 4 Dundee were the visitors at Celtic Park when goals from Tommy Johnson and Johan Mjallby secured a 2-1 win and Johnson struck again against St Mirren on April 7 to clinch the title and turn Celtic Park into an electric fun house.

"At the end of the game everyone was shouting and screaming and singing," said Lubo, "so it was a bit hard to take it all in. You don't really realise the significance of it all. But later on, when you put the videotape on and show your close friends and family the game, it's then the realisation and feeling of pride sinks in.

"Waking up the following morning is nothing special, you don't walk around the area with chest puffed out proclaiming 'I've won the Championship' or anything like that. You don't wake up with the feeling that it was all a dream, it's just simple, it happens. I honestly felt more pride after the matter when I was able to go to Slovakia and show the tape over there and share it with family and friends."

The trophy was presented two weeks later at Celtic's next home game against Hearts and the Bhoys won by a single goal scored by, yes you've guessed it, Lubo Moravcik the scourge of the Tynecastle side. There was still one more Rangers game yet to play and on April 29 Celtic visited Ibrox knowing that the title was in the bag and there was only pride to play for, if 'only' is a word that can be used in any Old Firm context.

The game was another classic though and a magnificent 3-0 victory for Celtic to put the icing on the cake with TWO supremely wonderful goals from Lubo and another equally awe-inspiring touch from Larsson to give him his 50th goal of the season.

"I remember shooting off the crossbar in an earlier game there and Henrik scored from the rebound," said Lubo, "so I was very close to scoring already and after I scored the two goals against Rangers here at Celtic Park I thought maybe I could score against them at Ibrox, that would be nice for my whole career at Celtic.

"So to score two at Ibrox was a bonus for me. Any goal is nice but to score against Rangers, and at Ibrox was special, especially the second goal because I scored a couple of goals like that in France and Slovakia when I feinted to my left and went right or vice versa and this is something I like to do. Everyone knows I do that, it's like when Henrik goes to score a goal. Everyone know he's very agile and he has the ability so it's a very good feeling."

It ain't over until the fat lady sings though and at this point she was just running through the scales in preparation for the big finale. More was still to come in the shape of the Scottish Cup but Lubo had sustained a knee injury and missed out on the final league game against Kilmarnock. There were serious doubts as to whether he would play in the final or miss out on the chance of yet another medal.

"I was just a bit unlucky," he recalled, "because I had a knee injury with a cut just under the joint and it was proving difficult to heal. I couldn't play in our previous match as the cut was deep and we had it stitched up but when I started the game I was a big risk. There was always the chance that it would open again. Unfortunately my first fall on the ground was crucial because the cut reopened and I couldn't continue in the game.

"But I knew even with the bandage I was a risk beforehand and I tried to play and couldn't finish it. Personally for me it was bad luck but altogether we won the game and

that was the important thing. So my week before the game was really uncertain."

So Lubo did make the final but when the cut reopened in the 18th minute he was replaced by Jackie McNamara who, just over 20 minutes later, scored Celtic's opening goal. Larsson added another two to take his goalscoring tally to an amazing 53 for the season and the much-awaited Treble party started in earnest.

"I was simply happy," said Lubo, "but there was a sense of relief for the fans and the hope and faith they had in us winning the Treble after so many years. I thought it was a fantastic achievement for this team in winning Celtic's third Treble in the history of the club. And for the first time in 32 years made it even more special.

"I was already involved in the history of the club by way of the biggest shame in the club's annals when we lost to Inverness Caley but now this instalment was more positive and I was happy to be able to delete this dishonour."

The fat lady was belting it out at the top of her voice now. Celtic had turned a 21-point deficit in the league in to a 15-point winning margin and lifted both cups.

"It was definitely my best season ever," said Lubo, "In the beginning it was not easy because again we had a new manager and I came in a little bit late last season and at 35 and I didn't have a lot of positive points on my side in the close season. But I knew I needed to be ready to show my capabilities if I got the chance. I waited for my opportunity and I tried my best to show the manager what I could do and I think after the good results and good atmosphere I appeared more in the team.

"When I had the chance I tried to do my best and I think I managed to show him that I was the player I thought I was. I won another three medals, I can say I was lucky in signing another one-year contract and Martin O'Neill has brought a lot of success to the club and I was delighted to be involved in that. I played a couple of games and saw this team working well, I tried to do my best and everything was fantastic last season.

"We worked hard and at the end of the day or the end of the season when you get success it is a good feeling and there is always satisfaction. It is our job to make the supporters happy and it was recompense for the effort we put in during the season."

He added: "It's difficult to analyse Martin's input in one sentence but I think he knew before he came here what he wanted to do. I think now looking back with hindsight after last season I can analyse that he built a really solid team and with the success we didn't ever turn the wrong way. We always built upwards better and better and this was important as we didn't reach a point where we started to stagnate and I think this progression is still an ongoing thing, it is not finished.

"Yes, picking up three winners' medals in one season after so long in the game was the highlight of my career but generally in football it's not a question of young, old, early or late it's just done and that's okay. If I had done this at the beginning of my career I would maybe have gone on and won more medals but at the end of the day it's better than nothing. I think the focus on this was because of my age but some older players are better than the younger ones and vice versa but in football you never know and you can't plan anything.

"You can't look too far ahead in this game as football can change in one month, one week even one game or even one refereeing decision."

Lubo also played his final international game during the Treble season, a phase of his professional life that most people thought he had given up on a couple of years earlier.
"Some people think that because I was out for a year-and-a-half I

had retired myself from the international team," he said, "but I just didn't get the call from the new coach.

"However, I returned for a couple of games and then I made the decision to retire because at my age the travel and all that goes along with international football including the recovery period wasn't so easy any more and I wasn't too happy with the last couple of games. My last Slovakian game was in September 2000 against Sweden with Henrik Larsson and Johan Mjallby in the side but I regret nothing, I think it was a very good decision to finish and leave me more time and energy to concentrate on Celtic."

If concentrating on playing for Celtic means more goals like the one he scored last season almost directly from a corner kick then that's good news for connoisseurs of the Beautiful Game. But did he mean to score that goal and would he try it again?

"I think if anybody says they aimed for the top corner from that position then they are lying. Certainly you have the chance and you want to try and score so you aim for the target but if it hits the top corner then you can thank God. There is always a bit of luck in these sort of things. If you want to score then you have to shoot and take the chance.

"It's not something I continually try on the training ground because in this position you tend to swing the ball because you see a good run from an attacker but if it finishes in the top corner then thank you very much. I haven't been tempted to try it since but maybe it's another one I will keep for my last game, you never know what is going to happen."

Through the eyes of team-mate Henrik Larsson

"I think it's a pity that I didn't know a little bit more about him before he came here because he is a fantastic footballer. If I knew then what I know of him now then I would have been trying to watch a little bit more of his games."

I had never really heard of him before he arrived in Glasgow and didn't recall seeing him play. I played against him in Sweden when we met Slovakia but I wasn't aware of him as a player before he came to Celtic. However, as soon as he took to the training field with Celtic I saw straight away that he was a good player.

Left foot, right foot, it didn't matter and he made his debut against Rangers and got two goals – I mean that's some debut but then once I saw him playing I changed my mind right away. He wasn't a good player he is a great player.

In his first Celtic game we beat Dundee 6-1 and he had a great assist for me there with the outside of his right foot just put across for me to score a goal. He's a great player but it was simple stuff. I very rarely read the press and didn't pay much attention to what was being said when Lubo first arrived but that was their opinion and he proved them all wrong.

Then came the biggest test of all with the arrival of the Old Firm game. It's always nice to be out on the pitch but when you play Rangers and you manage to beat them 5-1 it's a great experience and I'm happy for Lubo that he made his Old Firm debut that way because it always makes it a little bit easier. People say that game played a big part in Lubo being accepted by not only by the Celtic supporters but by the press, but I think Dr Jozef Venglos knew exactly what he bought and he did a lot of good things for the club. He brought Lubo in so I mean he knew all along what he had been buying.

It's always like that when you come as a new player and you have to prove yourself and I think that counts for wherever you go in the world. Lubo has not only proved himself on and off the field but he is an ideal role model for any youngster starting off in the game. He is utterly professional in his fitness training and honing his skills so I can't see any better role model than that.

And on the field it is definitely a bonus knowing that Lubo is playing behind you and supporting the front line. It's always good to have him there because he can spot your run, pinpoint you and put you in with either foot - also he can win you the games and that's always important to have.

Many of our games have been won by his expertise from dead-ball situations and apart from Lubo and myself, we have Stilian Petrov and Alan Thompson who also noted for scoring from these positions. People do ask how we decide who will take the kick but it depends really on where it is. If it is really close we try to get Stilian in but it depends on the situation. In our recent game against Motherwell at Fir Park Lubo just felt like taking it so he took it and scored a fantastic goal.

We generally don't change things at the last second, we stand there and have a chat over the ball then decide what to do. I might back off or do a fake, or maybe take a shot myself but if you have two great feet like Lubo then most of the time he takes them.
To be honest we don't practice these things very much on the training field. Some moves are but most of them are improvised. When you see some of Lubo's free kicks it makes you wonder why we didn't know about him before he came to Celtic.

I know that he is well known in France and obviously Slovakia and the Czech Republic but it is a travesty that he wasn't really known elsewhere until recently. It's always hard, he got about 80 caps so he is obviously known but we hadn't heard so much about him here because he had been playing with lesser-known teams in France and then he went to Germany.

I think it's a pity that I didn't know a little bit more about him before he came here because he is a fantastic footballer. If I knew then what I know of him now then I would have been trying to watch a little bit more of his games.

Celtic could be the ideal stage for any player because there is a lot of attention up here so to be honest I think Lubo knew in himself he was a good football player so I don't think that he felt he had to prove something when he came here. But obviously as a player you always like to show that you are capable of playing at this level. And Lubo can do that with ease as he has a real appetite for the game and that doesn't surprise me despite his age.

I know some players fall away from the game earlier but Lubo has had his fair share of injuries too in his career and I think that helps you to motivate and really enjoy the game in which you are playing. And that is just one of the things that makes Lubo the player he is. He is definitely one of the best players I have ever played with, there's no doubt about that.

Henrik Larsson, 30, is the current holder of the Golden Shoe Award, which is given to Europe's top goalscorer, having scored a total of 53 goals in Celtic's Treble-winning season. The Swedish striker was also a bargain buy like Lubo, joining the club from Feyenoord for just £650,000.

THE FINAL SEASON

Did you have any heroes outside football?

"Not really. There are so many important people in the world it's difficult to pick just one person but I didn't have many interests outside football."

And so to the final chapter not just of this book but of a supremely wonderful playing career that has climaxed at Celtic Park and delighted any Celtic fan who has had the privilege to witness Lubomir Moravcik in action. There is still the rest of season 2001/2002 to go but the man is going out on a high with a clutch of Treble medals in his back pocket and finally appearing on the ultimate European club stage – the UEFA Champions League.

It is a fitting end for a player who only a few years ago was completely unknown to any of us and now we have been totally enlightened by his presence in a Celtic shirt. He was last year's OPTA Stats Scottish Player of the Year, this season he has been inducted into the Celtic Hall of Fame, he is also this year's Guest of Honour at the Annual Celtic Supporters' Association Rally – an accolade that is only bestowed upon true Celtic greats.

He played and scored for a FIFA World XI in a game in honour of Nelson Mandela in South Africa. His praises have been sung from on high by celebrities as diverse as the world's No.1 footballer Zinedine Zidane and the late Cardinal Thomas Winning who was the spiritual leader of all Scottish Catholics until his death in the summer of 2001.

Indeed, the Cardinal who had been watching Celtic since the 1930s went so far as to say that Lubomir Moravcik was the BEST Celtic player he had ever seen. There is a new generation of kids at Celtic Park who think that a corner kick is called a 'Lubo' because of the chants that reverberate around the stadium every time the team earn one.

ntl:
XARA

He is the model professional that every club wishes they had but he plays in the green and white of Celtic and for that we can be eternally grateful, but it would seem that this is his final season and he really is going out at the top so as he is a man who takes nothing for granted and a man who really does take each game as it comes and is as modest and self-effacing as they come we can only sincerely hope he takes some self-satisfaction from his time at Celtic and that he utterly enjoys his final months in the game that he truly loves.

He has again been a star performer in his final season and his spectacular goal in Ryan Giggs' recent testimonial was another to behold as Celtic defeated the English Champions 4-3. As far as the big stage goes, they don't some much bigger than Old Trafford, but where does that goal rate in his scrapbook of golden memories?

"We have to recognise that this was just a friendly with nothing at stake," he said, "but just to play at Old Trafford was a fantastic feeling and I thought if I could score it would be more of a souvenir for me. It was very nice to score just for this reason because I won nothing but personal pride and happiness, but it wasn't just Old Trafford or Manchester United but I also scored against Fabian Barthez, the best goalkeeper in the world from long range so altogether it was an amazing experience. A nice moment and great occasion but it was a friendly and nothing more important than pleasure – just a little pleasure in my life."

But how does Lubo feel to be going out on a high after so many years of relative anonymity?

"If we could win the Treble and the Champions League as well that would be a very nice finish! But what I really expect this season is to do well in the Champions League and massive concentration on the title fight in Scotland In the Championship last season we played it game by game and got better game by game until we won it but the Champions League is much more of a long-term battle. In the league we can improve on a game to game basis but in European football we have to do it season by season so we have already improved on last year's showing and we have to take that a stage further next term.

"It's a gradual process and it's something we have to be realistic about. There is no use rushing into it only to face massive disappointment as we are in a learning curve at the moment and that is the important thing for Celtic."

He added: "Playing in the Champions League was a very important factor in me deciding to play on for another year but I'll always remember when I was young that I always put some target before me, to make the first team, to play for the national team, to play in the European Championships, to play in the World Cup.

"And now with Celtic I had the opportunity to play in the Champions League, I said to myself I would like to see if I can compare with the best players and the best teams in Europe. This has become a personal challenge for me."

And on personal challenges for the future he added: "I definitely want to earn my coaching license and one day maybe if I get the opportunity I would like to manage a team.
"I'm definitely going to live in France, that is important for my children to continue their schooling there but after I do the license I don't know exactly where I will end up."

There has also been talk of him teaming up with Dr Jo in Celtic's European coaching/scouting operation. He said: "First of all I have to do my license and after that we will see what happens because I think it's almost two years to get this license and if I want to do that I have to be eligible."

There is no doubt that once Lubo does earn his coaching badge he will be courted by top teams throughout Europe and beyond as his inclusion in 1999's FIFA World XI against the Mandela XI would testify.

"That was great. I was always lucky in football," he recalled, "and that was just one special moment in my life, my football life. It was fantastic to score a goal for that FIFA team playing alongside the best players in the world, it was a great moment and a great souvenir."

Another keepsake must be when Zinedine Zidane was quoted on TV raving about Lubo.
"This came about because I had a good reputation in France and he could remember me. He said I'm not a Maradona or a Platini but I had the qualities of Hagi for example, but I didn't play in so many high-profile games, play for such big teams or earn the same sort of respect in Europe as Hagi"

And when Cardinal Winning was asked who was the best player he had ever seen in the hoops the answer fired back as quick as a flash was "Lubo Moravcik.
"As a youngster, it was Jimmy McGrory and you could mention Jimmy Delaney, Jimmy Johnstone, even Henrik Larsson. But the best all-rounder I've ever seen is Moravcik."

Lubo said: "That was a pleasure for me to hear that from such a distinguished man who has seen many great Celtic players down through the years. Obviously it's always better to hear positive things about yourself than negative. I mean looking back at the Inverness Caley game I was part of the biggest shame in the history of the club but I can tell you it will be much better to be remembered as the guy who helped win the Treble, you don't always court pleasure in this game."

Such is the humility of the man that when he attended the recent Celtic Hall of Fame he thought he was there as a member of the audience, not to pick up an award for being voted by the supporters among the top 100 Celts of all time.

"I didn't think I would get something," he said, "I just went along to say hello. Henrik wasn't feeling well and wanted to

leave so I said okay, I'll go with you as we live quite near each other. But they called me back and said I couldn't leave as I was being presented with an award. It was a fantastic honour. I do my job because it is my job to earn money for my family but to get this award and this honour was something really special. You look on it as a form of recognition and that gave me a great feeling."

There have been many great feelings at Celtic Park lately and Lubo along with his team-mates have played major parts in most of them but what does he think has been the most significant change in Celtic over the last season or so and how has the squad improved in both skill and team spirit departments?

"I think Martin brought quality everywhere. You've got a good atmosphere in the dressing room and you've got good training as well and these are vitally important. We don't have a lot of injuries and any players Martin has brought to the club have all brought positive aspects. I think Martin was the most important signing. He changed the situation by bringing stability and progress. We are still in progress and we do have self belief.

"You know, sometimes in Slovakia the coaches will say, 'my team can play well and they are good players but they don't have the confidence' It is the coach's job to give confidence and Martin, he was able to give us that confidence

and a system to breed self belief. Because we work with a system where everyone has his role and is confident in his own ability to perform that role. This is a job for the manager and that is one of the reasons why Martin is a big part in this success."

At some time or another we all wonder what it would be like to turn back the clock, revisit the past and muse on whether we would make any changes or not. The contemplation is purely hypothetical of course but if your average Celtic supporter stood and surveyed the magnificent stadium that is Celtic Park he may wonder if all this would have been possible if Celtic had indeed been more successful during the lean years.

Would we have accepted our lot then and carried on happily with what little we had because we had won a title here and there to totally obliterate any thoughts of Rangers threatening our cherished nine-in-a-row record. Would that average Celtic supporter have changed anything?

There is the tale of two men who travel back in a time machine and they are warned not to interfere with anything in the past, they are roundly cautioned not to even TOUCH anything lest disaster would befall on their return. They accept the warning and travel back to medieval times and land in the middle of a wood. They were in the wood for barely 30 seconds before returning but in that short time a butterfly fluttered past and one of the men automatically thrust out his hand and caught the butterfly immediately killing it.

The two men went back in to the machine and returned to their own present day. However, on alighting the machine at the other end they were shocked to find that everything in their own time had completely changed. The architecture was totally different, clothes were different, money was different, the government was different, the people spoke a different language and of course their colleagues were nowhere to be seen.

The essence of the story is that by killing the butterfly they had totally changed the whole course of history. If the butterfly was allowed to fly on it would have eventually been caught by a bird. The bird having been fed would have returned to its nest and on the way there would have been brought down by the arrow of the King. The King would then return to his keep satisfied with his day's hunting and everything would have been alright.

But because of the interaction of the time travellers the bird never caught the butterfly, the bird then didn't return to its nest at the allotted time and the King travelled further to satisfy his need to hunt only to be killed by bandits. Hence the complete change in the country some 700 years later.

So would that average Celtic supporter change anything if he were able to return say to Celtic's centenary season? Looking at the stadium as it is now the practical man in him would probably say no, don't tamper with what's gone before, but the dreamer in him would have been tempted to phone then manager Billy McNeill with the advice to get the butterfly net out, travel to Nitra and at all costs sign a 22-year-old Slovakian boy named Lubomir Moravcik. Better late than never, Moravcik did arrive at Celtic Park and he has enjoyed life in Scotland.

"My time here is not finished yet," he said, "but I'm sure that when I do leave I'll be able to look back and say I've really enjoyed my time here, I'm really proud about me and about what I've done at Celtic and I've also got to say that I was very lucky."

A LIFE LESS ORDINARY

Lubo dedicated this book to his father, a profound influence on his life and on his career, and the loss of his father is something which still affects him.

"I still miss my father, even more so now than before," he confessed. "Now that I have children of my own, I feel that if I could talk with my father we'd have much more to say to each other than before and I'd like to hear his opinion about a lot of things. I don't know how others reconcile themselves with such a loss, but for me it's very difficult. He would always advise me, tell me what to do. I would listen to him and he never let me down in anything. But what can I do now that he's dead? It's terribly sad but I can't do anything about it now.

"My father's main influence on me was that he always pushed me to get a good education. He insisted that I go to university and get a degree. "If you're a good footballer on the side, even better," he used to tell me.

"When he got ill I tried to help him and arranged specialist treatment for him in St. Etienne but looking back, I'm not sure I did the right thing. It may be that, unintentionally, I made it worse for him. I took him out of his familiar environment, away from the rest of the family, his friends, his old doctors. In circumstances like his, a change of environment can be very stressful. I wanted to help him but, instead, I caused him stress. I think it was a mistake, but I did what I thought was the best thing, according to my experience at that time. I brought him to France because I thought in western Europe he could get better care. I didn't realise that in many ways medical care in our country is just as good and the doctors are often better.

"I know that today I'd do something else completely. I'd stop playing and tell the club: "Sorry, I'm finished with football. My father's ill and I'm going to stay with him in Slovakia and do everything to help

him until he recovers." I'm sure that's what I'd do today. No-one would stop me. I was younger then. My father died, we buried him and a week later I was back playing. Should I have stopped playing football then and let it all go? I don't think my father would have wanted me to do that."

If Lubomir Moravcik has lived a life less ordinary, then he has also lit up the ordinary lives of countless fans in Slovakia, France and Scotland who have had the privilege to see him play. The player, himself, remains modest about his achievements and how he wants to be remembered.

"What do I wish for most?" reflected Moravcik. "For all the fans to remember, after I've gone, that I once played here and when they recall my name, to remember that I played well."